The Grammar Handbook 1

A handbook for teaching Grammar and Spelling

Sara Wernham and Sue Lloyd

Illustrated by Lib Stephen

Edited by Rachel Stadlen

Second Edition

Jolly Learning Ltd

Published March 2000
Reprinted 2001, 2005
Second edition published 2007

Jolly Learning Ltd
Tailours House
High Road
Chigwell
Essex
IG7 6DL
United Kingdom

Tel: (+44 or 0) 20 8501 0405
Fax: (+44 or 0) 20 8500 1696

Printed and bound in England.

The Photocopy Sections in this book use 'Sassoon Infant', a
typeface designed for children learning to read and write.

*The front cover shows two children doing the action for
verbs in the past tense.*

*The page numbers in this book have been kept within the
binding, at the base of each page, so that the numbers do
not appear on copies of the photocopiable pages.*

ISBN 978 1 870946 85 8

Acknowledgements

Our sincere thanks go first to Professor Alice Coleman, whose work has been an inspiration to us, and a profound influence on this project.

We are grateful also to Trudy Wainwright and the staff of St. Michael's Primary School, Stoke Gifford, as of course to our colleagues at Woods Loke Primary School. Their hard work and support in testing our material has greatly benefited this book.

Finally we would like to thank Jennifer Chew O.B.E., whose expertise has been invaluable.

Contents

PART 1

PART 2   Photocopiable material

Extra Activities

Introduction

The Grammar Handbook 1 is designed to follow *The Phonics Handbook*. It is intended to:

- introduce the rudiments of grammar,
- teach spelling systematically,
- improve vocabulary and comprehension,
- reinforce the teaching in *The Phonics Handbook*, and
- extend the children's phonic knowledge.

The teaching is multisensory, active, and progresses at a challenging pace. It is especially suitable for young children. Each part of speech, for example, is taught with its own action and colour. The actions enliven the teaching, and make the learning easier. The colours, which are useful for identifying parts of speech in sentences, match those used by Montessori Schools. Like *The Phonics Handbook*, *The Grammar Handbook 1* provides all the essential teaching ideas. It can be used alone, or with the valuable support of the *Jolly Grammar Big Book 1*.

Children's achievement

The most dramatic improvements to result from using *Jolly Grammar* will be found in the children's writing. The children will spell and punctuate more accurately, use a wider vocabulary, and have a clearer understanding of how language works.

In their first year at school, *Jolly Phonics* teaches children to write independently, by listening for the sounds in words and choosing letters to represent the sounds. This enables the children to write pages of news and stories. It is a joy to read their work and to see the great pride and confidence they derive from their newly-acquired skill. However, it is important to build on this foundation in the following year. *Jolly Grammar* provides teaching ideas for developing writing skills. The children become more aware that they are writing for a purpose: that their words are intended to be read and understood. They learn that writing is easier to understand if it is grammatically correct, accurately spelt, well-punctuated and neatly written – and that if the words used are interesting too, their writing can give real pleasure. Even in the early stages, it is valuable for children to have a simple understanding of this long-term goal.

The format of *The Grammar Handbook 1*

The programme consists primarily of photocopiable activity sheets for two lessons a week. Each lesson is designed to to be about one hour in duration, and material is provided for 36 weeks. Teaching ideas are offered alongside each activity sheet.

There are two elements to the programme, namely spelling and grammar. Each week the first lesson is devoted to spelling and the second to grammar. These terms are loosely used, and there is some overlapping: punctuation, vocabulary development and alphabet work are among the areas covered in both spelling and grammar lessons. This is deliberate; when mixed together, the two elements complement each other.

The teaching is intended to be envisaged as part of a broader literacy programme. If two days' literacy sessions are devoted to *Jolly Grammar* each week, this leaves three for other areas, such as comprehension, group reading, independent and creative writing, and handwriting practice. The children should be shown how spelling and grammar relate to their other work, in comprehension exercises, reading, and independent writing. For instance, if they have recently covered compound words, and there is an example of one in the poem they are studying, the children should be encouraged to look for it.

The teaching ideas alongside each activity sheet give useful suggestions and reminders. More detailed explanations and advice are provided in the two chapters following: 'Teaching ideas for Grammar' and 'Teaching ideas for Spelling'.

To avoid confusion, *Jolly Grammar* follows the convention of using different symbols to distinguish between letter names and letter sounds. Letter names are indicated by the symbols ‹ ›, e.g. 'Ship' begins with the letter ‹s›. By contrast, letter sounds are indicated by the symbols / /, e.g. 'Ship' begins with the /sh/ sound.

Teaching ideas for grammar

The benefits of learning grammar are cumulative. In the first instance, a knowledge of grammar will help the children improve the clarity and quality of their writing. Later it will also help them to understand more complicated texts, learn foreign languages with greater ease, and use Standard English in their speech.

Spoken language is living and varies from region to region. The grammar we first learn, through our speech, varies accordingly. However, sometimes there is a need for uniformity. This uniformity improves communications, and is one of the main ways of uniting people in the English-speaking world. An awareness of this helps children who do not speak Standard English to understand that the way they speak is not wrong, but that it has not been chosen as the standard for the whole country. The children need to learn the standard form of English, as well as appreciating their own dialect.

In their first year of *Jolly Grammar*, the children begin to develop an understanding of how their language works, and are taught some of the accepted grammatical conventions. The teaching aims to give an elementary understanding that we speak and write in sentences, and that the words we use fall into categories. The categories are known as parts of speech (sometimes also known as 'word classes'). Those introduced in *The Grammar Handbook 1* are nouns, pronouns, verbs, adjectives and adverbs. The children learn to use verbs to indicate whether something is happening in the past, present or future.

The term 'grammar' is used broadly with children of this age. Definitions of the parts of speech, and of what constitutes a sentence, have necessarily been simplified to age-appropriate 'working definitions'. As the children grow older, the definitions can be expanded and refined.

With all teaching there must be a degree of repetition. This is particularly so when teaching a new discipline like grammar. Every lesson should include some revision. Suggestions for revision are provided in the teacher's notes alongside the activity sheets. However, teachers should feel free to use their own judgement as to which areas their children need to revise.

Proper Nouns

A noun denotes a person or a thing. There are four kinds: common nouns (e.g. 'a toy'), proper nouns (e.g. 'Matthew'), abstract nouns (e.g. 'kindness') and collective nouns (e.g. 'the team'). *The Grammar Handbook 1* begins by introducing proper nouns, since the children are already indirectly familiar with them through their own names. Children like to work with their names, and already know that they start with a capital letter.

A proper noun is the particular name given to a:
• person, including their surname and title;
• place: e.g. river, mountain, park, street, town, county, country, continent, planet;
• building: e.g. school, house, library, swimming pool, cinema; and
• date: e.g. day of the week, month, religious holiday.

Proper nouns start with a capital letter. When we refer to people, places, days, etc. by their proper names, we use capital letters: for example, we use capital letters for 'Anna', 'Mount Everest' and 'Monday', but not for 'girl', 'mountain' or 'tomorrow'. The capital letters indicate that the name is important. Children can understand that they are themselves important, since they are unique, and that this is why their own name starts with a capital letter.

Action: The action for a proper noun is to touch one's forehead with the index and middle fingers. This is the same action as that used for 'name' in British Sign Language.

Colour: The colour for nouns is black.

Common Nouns

Only concrete nouns are taught in *The Grammar Handbook 1*. Abstract nouns (e.g. 'happiness') are more difficult for young children to grasp.

Everything we can see has a name by which we can refer to it. The children enjoy looking in the classroom for examples of objects, such as 'table', 'chair', 'desk', 'light', 'carpet', 'ruler', 'pencil'. As these names are not specific to any one object, but refer to tables, chairs, etc. in general, they are called common nouns and not proper nouns. At this stage the children find it useful to think of nouns as the names for things they can see and touch. To help the children decide if a word is a noun, they can see whether it makes sense to say the word 'a', 'an' or 'the' before it, e.g. 'the table', 'a chair', 'an elephant', etc. ('A', 'an' and 'the' are the three articles, which are explained later.)

Action: The action for a common noun is to touch one's forehead with all the fingers of one hand.

Colour: The colour for nouns is black.

In general children understand the concept of nouns easily, and have no trouble when asked to think of examples. Identifying nouns in sentences is more difficult, but comes with practice. In any spare moments, encourage the children to identify the nouns in sentences on the board, or in big books.

Plurals

Most nouns change in the plural, i.e. when they describe more than one. *The Grammar Handbook 1* introduces two regular ways the plural can be formed. The first is by adding an <s> to the noun, as in 'dogs', 'cats', 'girls' and 'boys'. The second applies to those nouns which end with ‹sh›, ‹ch›, ‹s›, ‹z› or ‹x›. These words usually form the plural by adding ‹es›, as in 'wishes', 'churches', 'kisses' and 'foxes'. When children listen carefully they can hear the different sounds produced by the ‹s› and ‹es› endings. The plural endings ‹s› and ‹es› often sound like /z/ and /iz/, as in 'dogs' and 'boxes'. Knowing that these words are plurals will help the children remember to spell the /z/ sound with an ‹s›.

Irregular, or tricky, plurals (e.g. 'children'), are not introduced in *The Grammar Handbook 1*.

Personal Pronouns

Pronouns are the little words used to replace nouns. *The Grammar Handbook 1* introduces the personal pronouns only. The relative pronouns (e.g. 'who'), possessive pronouns (e.g. 'mine' and 'my') and reflexive pronouns (e.g. 'myself') can be taught when the children are older.

Without pronouns, language would become boring and repetitive. To illustrate this, give the children an example of a story without pronouns, e.g. 'Jenny, John and Mary decided to go to the zoo. Jenny, John and Mary prepared the food and then Jenny, John and Mary set off.' With the pronoun 'they', this kind of repetition can be avoided. Examples of this sort help the children to understand the function of pronouns. They can appreciate why the word 'pronoun' has the word 'noun' in it, once they recognise that pronouns replace nouns.

There are eight personal pronouns:

I	(first person singular)
you	(second person singular)
he	(third person singular)
she	(third person singular)
it	(third person singular)
we	(first person plural)
you	(second person plural)
they	(third person plural)

Although in modern English the second person pronoun 'you' is used for both singular and plural, this is not the case in many foreign languages. In order to make learning such languages easier later on, *Jolly Grammar* introduces children to the distinction between 'you' used in the singular and 'you' used in the plural.

Actions:	I	–	point to self
	you	–	point to someone else
	he	–	point to a boy
	she	–	point to a girl
	it	–	point to the floor
	we	–	point in a circle to include self and others
	you	–	point to two other people
	they	–	point to the next-door class

Colour:	The colour for pronouns is pink.

Verbs

A verb says what a person or a thing does, and can describe an action, an event, a state or a change. It is easiest for children to think of verbs as 'doing words' at first. Ask each child for an example of something they do, with the word 'to' before it, so that they give verbs in the infinitive form, e.g. 'to run', 'to hop', 'to sing', 'to play', etc. This is not something they find difficult.

Since verbs in English are very complicated, *The Grammar Handbook 1* introduces only the simple tenses. For the verb root 'cook', for instance, the infinitive is 'to cook', the simple present tense is 'cook', the simple past tense is 'cooked', and the simple future is 'will cook'. Later, when the children learn the continuous and perfect modes of the verb, they can be told that the verbs they first learnt were known as the simple tenses. For reference, the table below shows all three modes in past, present and future:

	Past	*Present*	*Future*
Simple	looked	look	will look
Continuous	was looking	is looking	will be looking
Perfect	had looked	have looked	will have looked

Technically there is no future tense in English since, unlike the past tense, the future is not formed by modifying the verb root itself. At this stage, however, it is helpful for the children to think of verbs as taking place in the past, present and future. The complexities are better left until they are older.

Action: The action for verbs is to clench fists and move arms backwards and forwards at sides, as if running.

Colour: The colour for verbs is red.

Conjugating verbs: in the present

The children can now learn to conjugate regular verbs. This means saying the pronouns in order, with the correct form of the verb after each. Demonstrate how to conjugate the verb 'to run' in the present tense, doing the pronoun actions:

> I run
> you run
> he runs
> she runs
> it runs
> we run
> you run
> they run

Encourage the children to notice how the verb changes after he, she and it: with regular verbs, an ‹s› is added to the root. This is called the third person singular marker.

Action: The action for the present tense is pointing towards the floor with the palm of the hand.

Conjugating verbs: in the past

The children need an understanding of what the past is. Initially it helps them to think in terms of what happened yesterday, e.g. 'Yesterday I jumped'.

The regular past tense is formed by adding the suffix ‹-ed› to the root of the verb. As many verbs have a 'tricky' or irregular past form, it is best to choose a regular verb to work with, rather than asking the children for suggestions. Some verbs with regular past tenses are 'to jump' (jumped), 'to cook' (cooked), 'to play' (played). Demonstrate how to conjugate a regular verb in the past tense, doing the pronoun actions:

> I cooked
> you cooked
> he cooked
> she cooked
> it cooked
> we cooked
> you cooked
> they cooked

Write this conjugation on the board, for the children to look at the verbs and see which letters have been added to the root in each case. They can discover for themselves that it is always the suffix ‹-ed›. If the root ends with an ‹e›, as in 'bake', this must be removed before the ‹-ed› is added. The ‹-ed› can be pronounced in one of three ways: /t/, as in 'slipped', /d/, as in 'smiled' or /id/, as in 'waited'.

Action: The action for the past tense is pointing backwards over the shoulder with a thumb.

Generally, if a verb has a so-called 'short vowel' sound, there must be two consonants between the short vowel and the ‹-ed› suffix. If there is only one consonant, this must be doubled. The following list shows examples of some verbs to which the doubling rule applies, and some to which it does not:

Only one consonant after the short vowel, so doubling rule applies		*No need to double because there are two consonants already*	
bat	batted	pick	picked
hop	hopped	hand	handed
pin	pinned	rest	rested
rip	ripped	lift	lifted
hug	hugged	wish	wished
trap	trapped	shift	shifted

The children gradually learn to apply this useful doubling rule.

Although only verbs with regular past tenses are introduced at first, it is not long before the children realise that some verbs have 'tricky pasts'. They may want to conjugate a verb of their own choosing, such as 'to run'. It is interesting how quickly some of the children realise that the past tense is not 'I runned, you runned,' etc. but 'I ran, you ran,' etc. Those children who are in the habit of regularising the past tense of irregular verbs in their speech (e.g. saying 'I runned') will gradually have to learn the standard irregular forms.

Conjugating verbs: in the future

The word 'yesterday' was used to help the children to understand the idea of the past. Similarly, thinking in terms of 'tomorrow' helps them to understand what the future is, e.g. 'Tomorrow I shall post my letter.'

With simple verbs, when we speak of future time we use verb root and add the auxiliary 'shall' or 'will'. 'Will' can be used with all the pronouns but 'shall' should only be used with 'I' and 'we', the first person singular and plural. Demonstrate how to conjugate a regular verb in the future, doing the pronoun actions:

I shall swim
you will swim
he will swim
she will swim
it will swim
we shall swim
you will swim
they will swim

Action: The action for verbs which describe the future is pointing to the front.

Adjectives

An adjective is a word that describes a noun or pronoun. At first it is sufficient to tell the children that an adjective describes a noun. Start by asking them to think of a noun, e.g. 'a pig'. Ask one child for a word to describe it, and say the two together, e.g. 'a pink pig'. Then ask another child for a second adjective, and add it into the phrase, e.g. 'a pink, noisy pig'. After several examples the children begin to understand how an adjective functions, especially when used directly before a noun.

When the children begin to apply this knowledge, their stories will become more interesting. Adjectives help the reader to imagine what is taking place.

Action: The action for an adjective is to touch the side of the temple with a fist.

Colour: The colour for adjectives is blue.

Adverbs

An adverb is similar to an adjective, but describes a verb rather than a noun. Usually adverbs describe how, where, when or how often something happens. They can also be used to modify adjectives or other adverbs, but the children do not need to know this at this stage. Start by asking the children to think of a verb, e.g. 'to swim'. Ask one child for a word to describe it, and say the two together, e.g. 'to swim slowly'. (When the verb is in the infinitive form, as here, it is usually better to put the adverb after the root 'swim', to avoid a split infinitive, as in 'to slowly swim'.) After several examples the children begin to understand how an adverb functions. At this stage it helps them to think of an adverb as being found next to a verb, and of often ending with the suffix ‹-ly›. Later, however, the children will discover many instances where this is not the case, and will need to refine their understanding.

Action: The action for an adverb is to bang one fist on top of the other.

Colour: The colour for adverbs is orange.

a / an / the

The words 'a', 'an' and 'the' are known as articles. 'A' and 'an' are used before singular nouns and are called the indefinite articles, as in 'a man' and 'an egg'. 'The' is used before singular and plural nouns and is called the definite article, as in 'the dog' and 'the boys'. The articles are a special sort of adjective.

Individual schools can decide whether or not to use the full terminology at this stage. While young children like learning new and difficult words, there is a limit to how many they can cope with at once. For most classes it is sufficient to refer to these words as 'articles'.

Children need to learn when to use 'an' instead of 'a'. As a simple rule of thumb, tell them to look at the word after the article. If the first letter is a vowel, then they should use 'an', e.g. 'an apple', 'an egg', 'an itch', 'an orange', 'an umbrella.' There are exceptions to this rule, however, which the children may notice. If a word starts with a 'long u' sound, as in 'unicorn' and 'union', the article is 'a'. This is because the 'long u' sound is in fact made up of two sounds, the first of which is the consonant /y/. The same thinking can be applied to words that start with a silent ‹h›. Since the consonant ‹h› is silent, the first sound that is actually heard is a vowel, so these words take the article 'an', e.g. 'an hour'.

Sentences

The full definition of a sentence is complicated, and more than children can cope with at this stage. However, because they speak in sentences, they already have a general sense of a sentence as expressing a complete thought. If each child is asked for one sentence of news about their weekend, the majority will be able to give one.

At this stage it is sufficient for the children to know that a sentence starts with a capital letter, ends with a full stop, and must make sense. Soon they will learn that it must also have a verb, and eventually that it must have a subject. Although they are not ready for this yet, it is still important that the children learn about sentences. This knowledge helps them organise their writing into manageable units, rather than linking one idea after another with the word 'and'.

Questions

The children need to understand what a question is and how to form a question mark correctly. If a sentence is worded so as to expect an answer, then it is a question and needs a question mark instead of a full stop. The children need to practice many examples before they remember this automatically. Practice saying sentences and having the children indicate whether or not they are questions. The children can answer by nodding their heads for 'yes', or shaking them for 'no'. Once this exercise becomes familiar the roles can be reversed, with the children thinking up the sentences.

Parsing: identifying the parts of speech in sentences

Parsing is identifying the function of words in sentences. Each word must be looked at in context to decide which part of speech it is. For example, the sentence 'Six boys swam quickly,' can be parsed as: adjective, common noun, verb, adverb.

Many words can function as more than one part of speech, e.g. 'light' can be the noun 'a light', the verb 'to light', or the adjective in 'a light colour'. It is only by analysing a word's use within a sentence that its function can be identified.

The children's ability to parse will develop gradually with regular practice. There are different ways to practise parsing. Start by writing simple sentences on the board for the children to identify the parts of speech. First ask the class, or one child, to read the sentence. Then point to one of the words and ask the children to call out which part of speech it is, or to do the appropriate action. Alternatively, ask individual children to come to the board, and find and underline particular parts of speech in the appropriate colours. Another possibility is to do the action for one of the parts of speech, and call on a child to find an example of it in the sentence, and underline it in the appropriate colour. Alternatively, have the class copy down the sentence and underline each part of speech in the appropriate colour.

Improving vocabulary and using a dictionary

The speed at which children acquire vocabulary varies enormously. Many children do not do so easily. They have to hear a given word a great many times before adopting it into their vocabulary.

We all use far fewer words in normal speech than we encounter in writing. The more a child reads, the greater the likelihood of their vocabulary improving. However, private reading alone is too haphazard a method to rely on, especially for those children without anyone at home who is willing or able to explain the meanings of unfamiliar words.

If a new word is introduced and defined for the children in the classroom, very are able to recall it or say what it means the following day. To learn the word, most children need to encounter it on several different occasions, practising saying it and verbally putting it into sentences themselves. A systematic approach to vocabulary teaching is therefore very important.

The Grammar Handbook 1 introduces many words that will be unfamiliar to the children. Obviously the grammatical terms themselves will be new to them. Probably some words from the spelling lists and activity sheets will be too. It is worth choosing a selection of words appropriate to the needs of a particular class, and teaching them systematically with enough repetition to ensure that they are mastered.

Young children who are able to read, and to decode new words, are fascinated by dictionaries. Once they are familiar with the alphabet and understand how the dictionary works, they enjoy finding words for themselves. Most children are capable of learning to use a dictionary designed for use in schools. Reading the meanings of the words they find improves the children's comprehension. This is a good habit which should be encouraged; the frequent practice of alphabet and dictionary work in *The Grammar Handbook 1* is designed to help the children acquire it.

When children first begin to write independently, their efforts should be encouraged regardless of the quality. However, after a year of writing freely, the children are ready to learn ways to improve their work. *The Grammar Handbook 1* encourages them to think of alternatives for words they commonly overuse, like 'said'.

Teaching ideas for spelling

Most children need to be taught to spell correctly. In *Jolly Grammar*, spelling is the main focus for one lesson each week.

There are a few children who learn to spell well through their reading. These children have a good memory for words. They teach themselves the code of English, mentally noting the different ways the sounds are represented as they read. When they come to write, these children use analogy to think how to spell unfamiliar words. Even when they are unsure of a spelling, they may be able to find it by writing the word in several ways and choosing the correct version. It does not necessarily follow that these children are more intelligent, or produce superior writing. It simply means that they have the necessary combination of attributes for accurate spelling, namely an excellent retentive memory for print, good phonological awareness and strong reasoning skills. When these children are explicitly taught the alphabetic code, they learn even faster.

Just as there are a few children who find it easy to spell accurately, there are some who find it exceedingly difficult. They often have spatial problems, a poor auditory/visual memory, or are inclined to muddle the sequence and direction of letters in words. It is important to identify a child's individual difficulty; whatever the problem, it has to be overcome. These children need a good grasp of phonics, and must recognise the need to work harder and with more self-discipline, if they are to achieve satisfactory results. Parental help is especially important for them.

Most children taught with *Jolly Phonics* in their first school are familiar with the vowel digraphs and the alternative ways of spelling the vowels sounds, but frequently do not know them by heart. The aim of the spelling work in *Jolly Grammar* is to reinforce the teaching that has gone before, as well as extending the children's knowledge.

The Grammar Handbook 1 teaches the following spelling features:

1. Vowel digraphs
2. Alternative spellings of vowels sounds
3. Plural endings
4. Short vowels and consonant doubling
5. Tricky words
6. Consonant blends

These six features are outlined in greater detail in the pages following.

1. Vowel digraphs

The children should already be familiar with the blending technique: 'If the short vowel sound doesn't work, try the letter name'. When reading words with an ‹i› spelling, for example, such as 'life', 'mind' and 'pipe', if the /i/ sound, as in 'sit', does not make sense, the children try the /ie/ sound, as in 'pie'. They can use the same technique with the other four vowels as well, which enables them to decode many unfamiliar words. However, this is a reading technique only, and will not help the children in their writing. For accurate spelling, they need a more thorough understanding of how the vowels work.

'Vowel digraph' is the term for two letters which make a single vowel sound, one or both of the letters being a vowel. Often the two letters are next to each other, e.g. ‹ay›, ‹ea›, ‹ou›, ‹oi›, ‹ew›. Two vowel letters are usually needed to make a so-called 'long vowel' sound, i.e. one of the vowel letter names: /ai/, /ee/, /ie/, /oa/ or /ue/. Generally the sound they make is that of the first vowel's name. Hence the well-known rule of thumb 'When two vowels go walking, the first does the talking'.

Sometimes the long vowel sound is made by two vowels separated by one or more consonants. In monosyllabic words, the second vowel is usually an ‹e›, known as a 'magic ‹e›' because it modifies the sound of the first. Digraphs with a magic ‹e› can be thought of as 'hop over ‹e›' digraphs: ‹a_e›, ‹e_e›, ‹i_e›, ‹o_e› and ‹u_e›. Once again, the sound they make is that of the first vowel's name; the magic ‹e› is silent. Children like to show with a hand how magic from the ‹e› hops over the preceding consonant and changes the short vowel sound to a long one.

This is an alternative way of making the long vowel sounds, as in such words as 'bake', 'these', 'fine', 'hope' and 'cube'. The children need to be shown many examples. It helps them to understand if a piece of paper is held over the ‹e›, and the word is read without it. For example, ‘pipe’ becomes ‘pip’, ‘hate’ becomes ‘hat’, ‘hope’ becomes ‘hop’ and ‘late’ becomes’ ‘lat’. It does not matter if, as in this last example, the children find themselves producing nonsense words; the exercise will still help them to understand the spelling rule. When looking at texts on the board or in big books, it helps the children to look for and identify words with a ‘magic ‹e›’.

As there are only a few words with the ‘‹e› hop-over ‹e›’ spelling, e.g. ‘these’, ‘scheme’, ‘complete’, and as they are rather rare, and usually found in complicated words, this spelling is not taught as one of the main alternatives for the long vowel sounds. However, it is worth introducing it to the class.

2. Alternative spellings of vowels sounds

The more complicated aspects of English spelling should be made so familiar to the children as to become automatic. For example, if the children read ‘The brave man stayed on the train,’ they should be able to identify the words with /ai/ sounds: the ‹a_e› in ‘brave’, the ‹ay› in ‘stayed’, and the ‹ai› in ‘train’. By regularly looking for this kind of spelling feature in texts on the board, or in books, the children learn to apply their knowledge in their reading and writing. It is those children who have such knowledge, and know how to use it, who make the greatest progress. It is important that all children acquire these skills. The spellings should be regularly revised with flash cards.

In *The Grammar Handbook 1*, the main focus is on the vowel sounds and their alternative spellings. The list below shows the first spelling taught for each letter sound and the main alternatives introduced:

First spelling taught for sound:	Alternative spellings of sound:	Examples of all spellings in words:
ai	a_e, ay	rain, came, day
ee	ea	street, dream
ie	igh, y, i_e	pie, light, by, time
oa	ow, o_e	boat, snow, home
ue	ew, u_e	due, few, cube
er	ir, ur	her, first, turn
oi	oy	boil, toy
ou	ow	out, cow
or	au, aw, al	corn, sauce, saw, talk

3. Plural endings

Plurals are introduced to the children in the grammar lessons. However, there is a direct spin-off into spelling. By recognising when a word is plural, children can avoid making errors like spelling 'ducks' as 'dux'. Knowing that words ending in ‹sh›, ‹ch›, ‹x›, ‹s› and ‹z› make the plural with an ‹es› ending, also helps the children to spell accurately.

4. Short vowels and consonant doubling

For almost every rule of spelling in English, there are some words which break it. However, some rules are pretty reliable, and make the children's learning easier. One of these is the doubling rule. Hundreds of words follow this rule and very few do not, so it is definitely worth teaching.

Consonant doubling is governed by the short vowels, so the children need to be able to identify short vowel sounds confidently. For an entertaining way of helping them listen for short vowels, a puppet such as the Inky Mouse puppet and a box can be used.

For /a/, put the puppet **a**t the side of the box.

For /e/, make the puppet wobble on the **e**dge of the box.

For /i/, put the puppet **i**n the box.

For /o/, put the puppet **o**n the box.

For /u/, put the puppet **u**nder the box.

Then the children pretend that their fist is the box and their hand is the puppet.

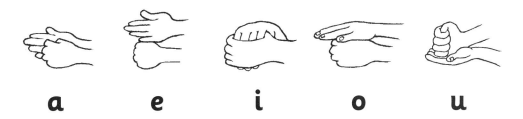

Start by calling out short vowel sounds. For each one, the children do the appropriate action with their hands. Then call out short words which have a short vowel, e.g. 'pot', 'hat', 'bun', 'dig', 'red'. The children should listen for the vowel sound in each word, and do the action. When most of the children have mastered this, progress to calling out short words with a variety of vowel sounds. For those which do not have a short vowel sound, the children must keep their hands still.

Activities like these help to keep the children 'tuned in' to identifying the sounds in words, as well as preparing them for the following rules:

Rules for consonant doubling:

a. In a short (i.e. monosyllabic) word with a short vowel sound, if the last consonant is ‹f›, ‹l›, ‹s› or ‹z›, this is doubled: e.g. 'cliff', 'bell', 'miss', 'buzz'.

b. In a short word with a short vowel sound, if the last consonant sound is /k/, this is spelt as ‹ck›: e.g. 'back', 'neck', 'lick', 'clock', 'duck'.

c. If there is only one consonant after a short, stressed vowel sound, this consonant is doubled before any suffix starting with a vowel, such as ‹-ed›, ‹-er›, ‹-est›, ‹-ing›, ‹-y›, as in. 'hopped', 'wetter', 'biggest', 'clapping' and 'funny'. Note that when ‹y› is a suffix, it counts as a vowel because it has a vowel sound. (This rule does not apply if the consonant is ‹x›, which is never doubled, even in words like 'faxed', 'boxing' and 'mixer'.)

In the case of the suffixes which begin with the letter ‹e›, it helps the children to think of the two consonants as forming a wall. If there were only one consonant, the wall would not be thick enough to prevent 'magic' hopping over from the ‹e›, and changing the short vowel sound to a long one. With two consonants the wall becomes so thick that the 'magic' cannot get over.

d. When a word ends with the letters ‹le›, and the preceding syllable contains a short, stressed vowel sound, there must be two consonants between the short vowel and the ‹le›. This means that the consonant before the ‹le› is doubled in words like 'paddle', 'kettle', 'nibble', 'topple' and 'snuggle'. No doubling is necessary in words like 'handle', 'twinkle' and 'jungle' because they already have two consonants between the short vowel and the ‹le›.

Young children tend not to grasp rules straight away, but learn them easily if the rules are regularly brought to their attention. As with many skills, success is dependent on constant repetition.

5. Tricky Words

The tricky words are a group of keywords which the children need to learn by heart. Most of them have irregular spellings. Although the others are phonically regular, the children need to memorise which spelling of the vowel sound they use. The first sixty tricky words are those introduced in *Jolly Phonics*. These need to be revised, and *The Grammar Handbook 1* includes two for revision each week. In addition, twelve new tricky words are introduced. A complete list of the seventy-two words is provided on page 194.

6. Consonant blends

It is worth devoting time to the consonant blends. They are phonically regular and so provide a reliable guide for both reading and spelling. Revision of initial and final consonant blends is provided in the grammar lessons, and each of the weekly spelling lists includes a regular word with a different consonant blend.

The children read unfamiliar words with greater ease once they can blend consonants together fluently, instead of sounding out each one on its own, e.g. '/dr/-/u/-/m/', not '/d/-/r/-/u/-/m/'. Flash cards of the blends should be used for regular practice. However, for writing, the children need to be aware of the individual sounds in a blend. They often write a word such as 'drum' as 'dum' because they do not hear the second sound in the blend. This problem can be overcome with regular practice. Call out blends and ask the children to say the individual sounds, holding up a finger for each one as they say it, e.g. for 'dr' they say /d/, /r/ showing two fingers, and for 'scr' they say /s/, /c/, /r/,' showing three fingers.

Improving spelling through phonic knowledge

Simply copying words does surprisingly little to improve the children's spelling. For example, some children write the day of the week on all their work by copying from a blackboard or wall chart. Yet even after years of doing so on a daily basis, many still cannot spell the days of the week without copying. If, however, the words are taught in more detail and practised without copying, the children are quite capable of learning to spell them. Each word needs to be analysed to see how it is made up, and a technique should be chosen to memorise any irregularities. For the days of the week, for example:

Monday	Use the 'Say as it sounds' technique, emphasising the short /o/ so that 'Mon' rhymes with 'gone'.
Tuesday	The children listen for, and say the sounds '/T/-/ue/-/s/-/d/-/ay/'. Ask them repeatedly how the /ue/ sound is spelt in 'Tuesday'.
Wednesday	Use the 'Say it as it sounds' technique, splitting the word into the syllables 'Wed-nes-day'.
Thursday	The children listen for, and say the sounds '/Th/-/ur/-/s/-/d/-/ay/'. Ask them repeatedly how the /er/ sound is spelt in 'Thursday'.
Friday	Use the 'Say as it sounds' technique, emphasising the short /i/ so that 'Frid' rhymes with 'rid'.
Saturday	Split the word into the syllables 'Sat-ur-day'. Ask the children repeatedly how the /er/ sound is spelt in 'Saturday'.
Sunday	This is the only day with a perfectly predictable spelling.

Once the days of the week have been taught, only give the initial letter when writing the date on the board. This encourages the children to practise what they have learned.

In spare moments when looking at texts with children, it helps to look closely at the spelling of some of the words. This develops the children's ability to apply their phonic knowledge to spelling. For example, if the word 'circus' comes up, (a) ask why the first ‹c› is soft and has a /s/ sound, (b) ask which spelling of the /er/ sound is used, and (c) point out that saying the last syllable – 'us' – as it sounds, helps with remembering the spelling. After a while, this analytic thinking becomes second nature to the children.

Photocopy Section 1

Grammar and Spelling Lesson Sheets

For each lesson there is a photocopiable activity sheet for the children to complete, accompanied by a page of teacher's lesson notes. The recommendations in the notes are intended to be followed systematically. However, if a suggestion seems inappropriate to a particular class situation, it can of course be adapted to suit.

All the lesson notes feature a notepad in the top right-hand corner. This shows a brief checklist of what to prepare for teaching, and is intended for easy reference once the teaching notes have been read. (Items which are useful, but not essential, are shown in brackets.)

The **grammar notes** all follow the same format:

a. Aim

b. Introduction

c. Main point

d. Grammar sheet

e. Extension activity

f. Rounding off

Each grammar lesson has its own particular focus, and the teacher's notes vary accordingly. However, the standard format helps to give the lessons a recognisable shape.

Contents of the sample notepad / lesson note image:

Prepare...
Big book to read
Grammar sheet 2
Scissors
Glue
(Extra 'Sentence Sticking': p. 205)

Grammar 2 – Sentence sticking

Aim: Develop the children's understanding of sentences.

Introduction: Explain that sentences help to organise words and to make the meaning of writing clear. Read a passage aloud, ignoring all the punctuation. Ask the children what is wrong. Ask them how they know where a sentence begins and ends. Read the passage again with the correct punctuation. Point out the capital letters and full stops at the beginning and end of the sentences.

Main point: Tell the children that sentences help organise spoken, as well as written, words. Ask several children each to tell the class one sentence of news. Choose one of the sentences and write it on the board.

Example: 'we went to the park'

Ask if this is a sentence, and if not why not. Put in the capital letter and full stop.

Grammar sheet 2: The children need to unscramble the words to make a sentence. Remind them to look for the capital letter to go at the beginning, and the full stop to go at the end. They can cut the words off the bottom of the sheet and stick them in the correct order in the spaces under the picture. It helps some children to move the words around physically. By cutting the words out and trying to put them in order, these children can be sure they are right before making a final decision. Alternatively the words can simply be written in the correct order in the boxes.

Extension activities: There are some more 'Sentence Sticking' Sheets on page 205. The children could also write some sentences of their own about the picture. The Writing Master on page 172 may be photocopied onto the back of the grammar sheets for the children to write on.

Rounding off: Go over the sheet with the class, so all the children can see if they got the sentence right. If there has been additional sentence sticking or writing, this can be shared with the rest of the class.

The **spelling notes** also follow a standard format:

a. Revision

b. Main point

c. Spelling sheet

d. Dictation

e. Spelling list

Two boxes at the bottom of each page show the words and sentences for dictation, and the weekly spelling list.

Many teaching points are common to all the spelling lessons, so these are explained in further detail below.

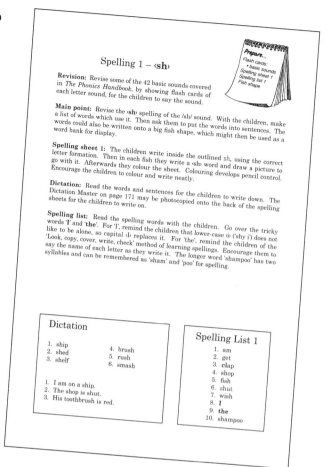

Spelling 1 – ‹sh›

Revision: Revise some of the 42 basic sounds covered in *The Phonics Handbook*, by showing flash cards of each letter sound, for the children to say the sound.

Main point: Revise the ‹sh› spelling of the /sh/ sound. With the children, make a list of words which use it. Then ask them to put the words into sentences. The words could also be written onto a big fish shape, which might then be used as a word bank for display.

Spelling sheet 1: The children write inside the outlined sh, using the correct letter formation. Then in each fish they write a ‹sh› word and draw a picture to go with it. Afterwards they colour the sheet. Colouring develops pencil control. Encourage the children to colour and write neatly.

Dictation: Read the words and sentences for the children to write down. The Dictation Master on page 171 may be photocopied onto the back of the spelling sheets for the children to write on.

Spelling list: Read the spelling words with the children. Go over the tricky words 'I' and 'the'. For 'I', remind the children that lower-case ‹i› ('shy i') does not like to be alone, so capital ‹I› replaces it. For 'the', remind the children of the 'Look, copy, cover, write, check' method of learning spellings. Encourage them to say the name of each letter as they write it. The longer word 'shampoo' has two syllables and can be remembered as 'sham' and 'poo' for spelling.

Prepare...
Flash cards:
• basic sounds
Spelling sheet 1
Spelling list 1
Fish shape

Dictation	
1. ship	4. brush
2. shed	5. rush
3. shelf	6. smash

1. I am on a ship.
2. The shop is shut.
3. His toothbrush is red.

Spelling List 1
1. am
2. get
3. clap
4. shop
5. fish
6. shut
7. wish
8. I
9. **the**
10. shampoo

a. Revision

Each lesson should start with a short burst of revision. In the early lessons, concentrate on the letter sounds, using flash cards. Over the course of the year, other areas can be added, e.g. consonant blends, identifying sounds in words, reciting the alphabet, and calling out the letter names of tricky words.

b. Main Point

The main focus of most of the spelling lessons is a digraph, one being featured each week. The children read and sound out words which use the digraph for that week. It is important to have available a set or list of regular words using each of the digraphs. For the /sh/ sound, for example, the list might include 'shop', 'ship', 'wish', 'fish', 'mesh', 'rash', and 'splash'. Many examples are provided in the *Jolly Phonics Word Book* and the *Jolly Phonics Blending Cards*.

c. Spelling sheet

The focus of each spelling sheet reflects the main teaching point, whether it is a digraph, a trigraph, or the short vowels. Always encourage the children to be accurate in their work and to colour neatly.

d. Dictation

As a weekly exercise, dictation is useful in a number of ways. It gives the children regular practice in listening for sounds in the words they write, and is a good way of monitoring their progress. It helps the children develop in their independent writing, and encourages the slower writers to increase their speed.

Each dictation list consists of six words and three simple sentences. These all revise the spelling introduced that week. For example, if the focus for a particular week is the ‹igh› spelling of the /ie/ sound, then the six dictation words usually feature it.

Begin by calling out the first word for the children to write down. Then ask one of them to sound it out, and as they do so, write the letters on the board. On reaching the sound of the week, the child should say the sound, e.g. /ie/, and then name the letters used to spell it, in this case ‹igh›. The other children check whether they have written the word correctly, and, if so, give themselves a tick. If there is time after the sentences have been dictated, check that the regular words in the sentences have been sounded out properly and the tricky words spelt correctly. Have the children say the names of the letters in the tricky words.

Dictation tends to go slowly at first, and it may be necessary to reduce the number of words and sentences. However, aim to go quite fast. When the majority of children have finished a word or sentence, go on to the next. The few children who have not finished should leave the item incomplete, and move on. This encourages them to get up to speed. For extra practice, these children could be given words for dictation homework. (Words may be selected from the Homework Writing Sheets in *The Phonics Handbook*.)

Most of the dictation words are regularly spelt. The children should be able to spell them correctly by listening for each sound and writing the letter(s) for it. This type of teaching helps the children to keep focused on sounds and prepares them for more advanced work with analogy and word patterns. Most young children are unable to use analogy for reading or spelling until they have been through the phoneme-blending stage and have a reading age of 7+ years.

Without regular practice, some children lose the ability to hear the sounds in words. These tend to be the children who were slowest to acquire phonemic awareness in the first place. It is easy to identify problems by looking at the children's independent writing. For example, if a child writes the word 'play' as 'paly', this usually indicates that the child needs to be taught to listen more carefully. Regular listening practice is particularly important for such children.

There are a number of activities introduced in *The Phonics Handbook*, which can be used to improve phonemic awareness with a class, group or individual, such as:

- holding up one finger for each sound in a word, e.g. four fingers for 'swing',
- orally 'chopping' sounds off a word, one by one, e.g. 'spot, pot, ot, t'
- splitting a word into onset and rime, e.g. 'str-eet',
- splitting a word into syllables, e.g. 'luck-y', and
- making new words by changing one sound at a time, e.g. 'pin, pip, ship, sheep'.

e. Spelling list

Each week the children are given ten spellings to learn for a test. It makes sense to give the spelling homework at the beginning of the week, and to test at the end of the week or on the following Monday.

The words have been carefully selected to enable every child to have some success, with the majority achieving full marks.

Words 1 and 2 in each spelling list are regular 2- or 3-letter words, and the third is also regular, but with a consonant blend. All the children

Spelling List 1
1. am
2. get
3. **clap**
4. shop
5. fish
6. shut
7. wish
8. **I**
9. **the**
10. shampoo

should be able to spell these correctly by listening for the sounds. Words 4, 5, 6, 7 and 10 generally feature the spelling of the week, and are usually regular. Number 10 is a longer word. The children need encouragement in tackling long words to build their confidence. Words 8 and 9 are tricky words that need to be practised by repeating the letter names, and using the 'Look, Copy, Cover, Write, Check' method (see pages 195-200). Allow a few minutes each day for reciting the letter names of these two words, especially with the children who normally fail to get full marks for their spelling homework. It is important to go over the words on the list during the spelling lesson. It is not enough simply to send home a list of words for the children to learn. At odd moments during the week ask the class, or individual children, to spell or sound out words from the list orally, or to test each other in pairs.

Each child takes the spellings home in a small vocabulary-size exercise book. In Photocopy Section 4 the spelling words are set out in the groups of ten, ready for photocopying. At the beginning of each week, stick the right section into each child's Spelling Homework Book. At this stage it is best not to ask the children to write the words into their books themselves because it is time-consuming and their writing is not always neat enough for their parents to read.

Test and mark the spellings each week. The results should be written in the Spelling Homework Book for the parents to see, shown either as a mark out of ten, or with a coded system if preferred. A coloured star system might be used, for example, with a gold star for 10/10, a silver star for 9/10 and a coloured star for 8/10. A letter of encouragement to parents is provided on page 187. Most parents like to be involved in the homework and are interested in how many words their child spelt correctly, and which words were mis-spelt.

Children need to be aware that accurate spelling is important for their future. There is no magic wand that can be waved to make them good at spelling. A certain amount of dedication and practice is needed.

Jolly Phonics introduced the children to three spelling techniques:

a. 'Look, Copy, Cover, Write, Check',
b. 'Say as it sounds', and
c. Mnemonics.

Jolly Grammar continues to encourage the use of these methods. Photocopiable sheets for practising the tricky word spellings with the 'Look, Copy, Cover, Write, Check' method are provided on pages 195-200.

Spelling 1 – ‹sh›

Prepare...
Flash cards:
• basic sounds
Spelling sheet 1
Spelling list 1
Fish shape

Revision: Revise some of the 42 basic sounds covered in *The Phonics Handbook*, by showing flash cards of the letter sounds. For each flash card the children say the sound.

Main point: Revise the ‹sh› spelling of the /sh/ sound. With the children, make a list of words which use it. Then ask them to make up sentences, using some of the words. The words could also be written onto a big fish shape, which might then be used as a word bank for display.

Spelling sheet 1: The children write inside the outlined sh, using the correct letter formation. Then in each fish they write an ‹sh› word and draw a picture for that word. Afterwards they colour the sheet. Colouring develops pencil control. Encourage the children to colour and write neatly.

Dictation: Read the words and sentences for the children to write down. The Dictation Master on page 171 may be photocopied onto the back of the spelling sheets for the children to write on.

Spelling list: Read the spelling words with the children. As a class, call out the sounds in the regular words, and say the letter names for the tricky words 'I' and 'the'. For 'I', remind the children that lower-case ‹i› ('shy i') does not like to be alone, so capital ‹I› replaces it. For 'the', remind the children of the 'Look, copy, cover, write, check' method of learning spellings. Encourage them to say the name of each letter as they write it. The longer word 'shampoo' has two syllables and can be remembered as 'sham' and 'poo' for spelling.

Dictation		Spelling List 1
1. ship	4. brush	1. am
2. shed	5. rush	2. get
3. shelf	6. smash	3. **clap**
		4. shop
		5. fish
1. I am on a ship.		6. shut
2. The shop is shut.		7. wish
3. His toothbrush is red.		8. **I**
		9. **the**
		10. shampoo

Write a ‹**sh**› word and draw a picture in each fish.

Action: Place finger over lips and say *sh, sh, sh.*

Grammar 1 – Rainbow Capitals

Prepare...
Alphabet poster
Grammar sheet 1
Coloured pencils
Alphabet Letter
Sets, pp. 202-3
(Any alphabet
games/puzzles)

Aim: Develop the children's ability to recognise and write capital letters. Develop their knowledge of the alphabet.

Knowing the alphabet is the first step towards being able to use word books, dictionaries and thesauruses.

Introduction: Say the alphabet with the children. There should be a copy available that they can see. Point to a letter and ask the children to say its sound. Repeat for other letters. The children need to know the order of the alphabet thoroughly. Throughout this term they should practise reciting it as often as possible.

Main point: Go over the formation of the capital letters. Always start at the top. The starting point for 'O' and 'Q' is slightly to the right, as if writing a letter 'C'.

Grammar sheet 1: The children write inside the outlined letters, using a coloured pencil. Then they have another go, writing the letters with a different coloured pencil. Their lines will cross over each other inside the outlines, but this does not matter. The children keep writing the letters using a different coloured pencil each time, until each letter is filled with its own 'rainbow'.

Extension activity: The children put letters into alphabetical order, using the Alphabet Letter Sets on pages 202-3. They could also use any alphabet puzzles available.

Rounding off: Give each child a different letter from one of the Alphabet Letter Sets. The children take turns saying the sound and/or name of their letter.

Rainbow Capital Letters

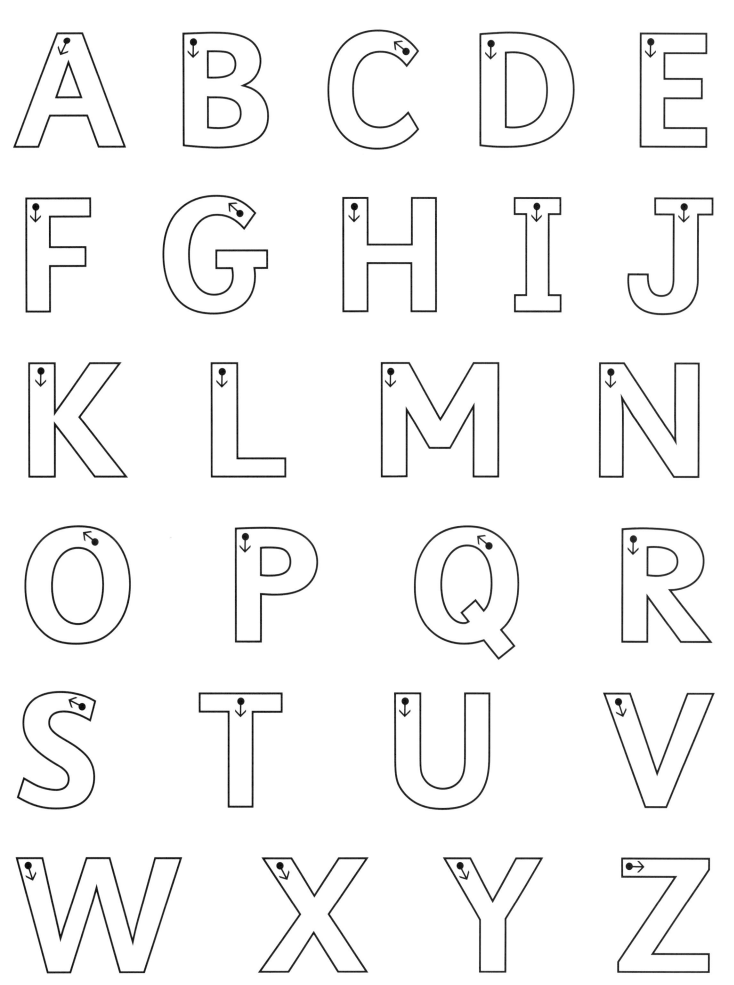

Spelling 2 – ‹ch›

Prepare...
Flash cards:
• basic sounds
• tricky words
Spelling sheet 2
Spelling list 2
Chest shape

Revision: Revise some basic sounds. Revise tricky words 'I' and 'the'.

Main point: Revise the ‹ch› spelling of the /ch/ sound.
With the children, make a list of words which use it. Then ask them to make up sentences, using some of the words. The words could also be written onto a big chest shape, which might then be used as a word bank for display.

Spelling sheet 2: The children write inside the outlined ch, using the correct letter formation. Then in each chest they write a ‹ch› word and draw a picture for that word. Afterwards they colour the sheet. Colouring develops pencil control. Encourage the children to colour and write neatly.

Dictation: Read the words and sentences for the children to write down. The Dictation Master on page 171 may be photocopied onto the back of the spelling sheets for the children to write on.

Spelling list: Read the spelling words with the children. As a class, call out the sounds in the regular words, and say the letter names for the tricky words '**he**' and '**she**'. The longer word 'chicken' has two syllables and can be remembered as 'chick' and 'en' for spelling. It helps the children remember the spelling if they emphasise the /e/ sound in the second syllable, pronouncing it to rhyme with 'pen'.

Dictation

1. chin
2. much
3. chop
4. bench
5. such
6. lunch

1. I am rich.
2. She sat on the bench.
3. He had chips for lunch.

Spelling List 2

1. if
2. hot
3. **bl**ot
4. chips
5. lunch
6. chest
7. much
8. **he**
9. **she**
10. chicken

Write a ‹**ch**› word and draw a picture in each chest.

chest

Action: Move arms at sides as if you are a train, saying *ch, ch, ch.*

Grammar 2 – Sentence sticking

Prepare...
Big book to read
Grammar sheet 2
Scissors
Glue
(Extra 'Sentence Sticking', p. 205)

Aim: Develop the children's understanding of sentences.

Introduction: Explain that sentences help to organise words and to make the meaning clear. Read a passage aloud, ignoring all the punctuation. Ask the children what is wrong. Ask them how they know where a sentence begins and ends. Read the passage again with the correct punctuation. Point out the capital letters and full stops at the beginning and end of the sentences.

Main point: Tell the children that sentences help organise spoken, as well as written, words. Ask several children to tell the class one sentence of news each. Choose one of the sentences and write it on the board, without punctuation.

Example: 'we went to the park'

Ask if this is a sentence, and if not why not. Put in the capital letter and full stop.

Grammar sheet 2: The children need to unscramble the words to make a sentence. Remind them to look for the capital letter to go at the beginning, and the full stop to go at the end. They can cut the words off the bottom of the sheet and stick them in the correct order into the spaces under the picture. It helps some children to move the words around physically. By cutting the words out and trying to put them in order, these children can be sure they are right before making a final decision. Alternatively the words can simply be written in the correct order in the boxes.

Extension activities: There are some more 'Sentence Sticking' Sheets on page 205-8. The children could also write some sentences of their own about the picture. The Writing Master on page 172 may be photocopied onto the back of the grammar sheets for the children to write on.

Rounding off: Go over the sheet with the class, so all the children can see if they got the sentence right. If any children have done additional sentence sticking or writing, ask them to share it with the rest of the class.

Sentences

Cut out the words.
Put them in order, to make a sentence about the picture.

pond.	A	duck
on	swims	the

Spelling 3 – ‹th›

Revision: Revise some basic sounds. Revise tricky words 'I', 'the', 'he' and 'she'.

Main point: Revise the ‹th› spelling of the voiced and unvoiced /th/ sounds. To help the children feel the difference between the voiced and unvoiced sounds, tell them to touch the front of their throats. With a voiced /th/ they will feel vibrations, whereas with an unvoiced /th/ they will not. With the children, make a list of words which use /th/. Then ask them to make up sentences, using some of the words. The words could also be written onto a big thought bubble shape, which might then be used as a word bank for display.

Examples: voiced /th/:   'this'   'that'   'then'
                    unvoiced /th/:   'thin'   'thick' 'three'

Spelling sheet 3: The children write inside the outlined th, using the correct letter formation. Then in each thought bubble they write a ‹th› word and draw a picture for that word. Afterwards they colour the sheet. Colouring develops pencil control. Encourage the children to colour and write neatly.

Dictation: Read the words and sentences for the children to write down. The Dictation Master on page 171 may be photocopied onto the back of the spelling sheets for the children to write on.

Spelling list: Read the spelling words with the children. As a class, call out the sounds in the regular words, and say the letter names for the tricky words '**me**' and '**we**'. The longer word 'thinking' has two syllables and can be remembered as 'think' and 'ing' for spelling.

Dictation	
1. this	4. thin
2. then	5. think
3. with	6. thick

1. That moth is big.
2. He is thin.
3. She cut the cloth.

Spelling List 3

1. us
2. sad
3. **flag**
4. this
5. with
6. that
7. thank
8. **me**
9. **we**
10. thinking

Write a ‹**th**› word and draw a picture in each thought bubble.

 Action: Pretend to be naughty clowns and stick out tongue a little for *th*, and further for *th*.

Spelling sheet 3

Grammar 3 – Sentences

Prepare...
Alphabet poster
(Jolly Grammar
Big Book 1)
Write up examples
Grammar sheet 3
(Alphabet Writing
Card, p. 204)

Aim: Develop the children's understanding of sentences.

Introduction: Help the children practise saying the alphabet. Use an alphabet poster, or the alphabet in the *Jolly Grammar Big Book 1*. Once they know it really well they will not need to look. Point to, or hold up letters (both capital and lower-case) and ask for their names and/or sounds. Ask which letter comes after the one being shown. The children find it easier to name this letter than the one which comes before. This is a good activity for any spare moments.

Main point: Explain that simply having a capital letter at the beginning of a line of writing, and a full stop at the end, does not make a sentence. The words in between must make sense too. (This is a very simple working definition of a sentence that young children can understand. As they gain in understanding it can be added to and refined.) Look at some incorrect sentences with the children.

Examples: 'the frog is green'
             'The cat ran up the.'

Ask why each line of writing is not a proper sentence. Correct them with the class.

Grammar sheet 3: The children read each line of text and decide whether it is a proper sentence. If they think it is correct, they copy the sentence underneath. If not they write the sentence correctly underneath.

Extension activity: The children practise writing the alphabet using the Alphabet Writing card on page 204.

Rounding off: Go over the sheet, with the class deciding if the sentences are correct. If they are not, ask the children why not, and do the corrections with them.

Are these sentences correct?

Write out each sentence correctly underneath.

1. the dog is spotty.

_____

2. The duck swims on the.

_____

3. I sleep in a bunk bed.

_____

4. i like fish and. chips

_____

5. He is playing football.

_____

Spelling 4 – ‹ng›

Revision: Revise some basic sounds. Revise tricky words 'I', 'the', 'he', 'she', 'me' and 'we'.

Main point: Revise the ‹ng› spelling of the /ng/ sound. Remind the children that it can go with all of the vowels, not just ‹i›. Practise saying 'ang', 'eng', 'ing', 'ong' and 'ung'. With the children, make a list of words which use each spelling. Then ask them to make up sentences, using some of the words. The words could also be written onto an enlarged copy of Spelling sheet 4, which might then be used as a word bank for display.

Spelling sheet 4: The children write inside the outlined ng, using the correct letter formation. Then in each ring they write an ‹ng› word and draw a picture for that word. Afterwards they colour the sheet. Colouring develops pencil control. Encourage the children to colour and write neatly.

Dictation: Read the words and sentences for the children to write down. The Dictation Master on page 171 may be photocopied onto the back of the spelling sheets for the children to write on.

Spelling list: Read the spelling words with the children. As a class, call out the sounds in the regular words, and say the letter names for tricky words '**be**' and '**was**'. For 'was', as well as saying the letter names as they write them, the children could use the 'Say it as it sounds' spelling method, pronouncing 'was' to rhyme with 'mass'.

Dictation

1. wing
2. song
3. bring
4. spring
5. sung
6. clang

1. The string was long.
2. She sang a song.
3. He had a sling on his arm.

Spelling List 4

1. in
2. leg
3. **gl**ad
4. ring
5. sang
6. strong
7. lung
8. **be**
9. **was**
10. length

Write an ‹**ng**› word and draw a picture in each ring.

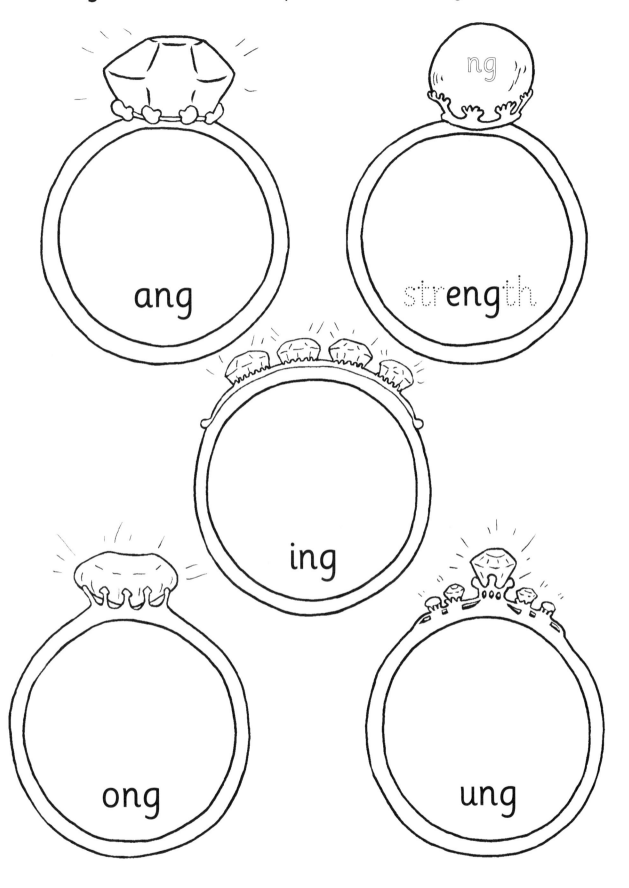

ang

strength

ing

ong

ung

Action: Imagine you are a weight lifter and pretend to lift a heavy weight above your head saying *ng...*

Grammar 4 – Capital letters

Prepare...
Alphabet poster
Grammar sheet 4
Alphabet letters
(Alphabet Letter
Sets, pp. 202-3)
(Alphabet Writing
Card, p. 204)

Aim: Develop the children's ability to recognise the capital and lower-case forms of each letter.

Introduction: Help the children practise saying the alphabet. Use an alphabet poster, or the alphabet in the *Jolly Grammar Big Book 1*. Once they know it really well they will not need to look.

Main point: Revise formation of the capital letters, especially those that are very different from the lower-case letters: 'A', 'B', 'D', 'E', 'F', 'G', 'H', 'M', 'N', 'Q', 'R', 'T' and 'Y'. Write or hold up letters (both capital and lower-case), and ask for their names and/or sounds. Then write or hold up a lower-case letter and ask one of the children to write its capital letter on the board. Repeat with other letters. This is a good activity for spare moments.

Grammar sheet 4: The children write the capital letters next to the lower-case letters. Then they join the capital and lower-case letters at the bottom of the sheet.

Extension activity: See how quickly the children can sort sets of letters into alphabetical order, using the Alphabet Letter Sets on pages 202-3. The Alphabet Writing Card on page 204 can be used for further practice.

Rounding off: From an alphabet set, give each child a different letter. Call out the alphabet slowly. When each letter is called, the child holding it stands up and moves to the front. The children at the front form an alphabet line, holding out their letters for the rest of the class to see. Once all the children come to know the alphabet better, this activity can be repeated with the children saying the names of their letters themselves.

Capital Letters

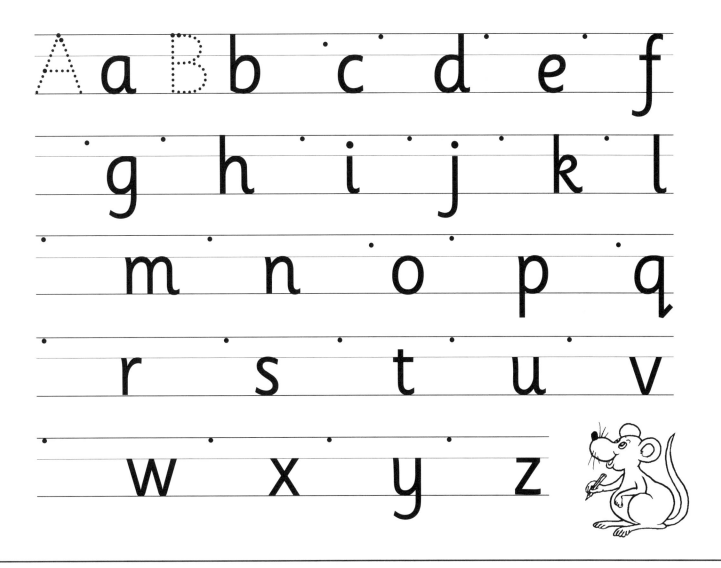

Aa Bb c d e f
g h i j k l
m n o p q
r s t u v
w x y z

Join each capital letter to its lower-case letter.

A   D   E   R
d   b   e
a   n   g   G
Q   r
N   q   B

Spelling 5 – ‹qu›

Prepare...
Flash cards:
• basic sounds
• tricky words
Spelling sheet 5
Spelling list 5
Duck shape

Revision: Revise some basic sounds. Revise tricky words 'I','the', 'he', 'she', 'me', 'we', 'be' and 'was'.

Main point: Revise the ‹qu› spelling of the /qu/ sound. Remind the children that ‹qu› is made up of two sounds /k/ and /w/. If the children hear /kw/ in a word, they must remember to write ‹qu›. With the children, make a list of words which use ‹qu›. Then ask them to make up sentences, using some of the words. The words could also be written onto a big duck shape, which might then be used as a word bank for display.

Spelling sheet 5: The children write inside the outlined qu, using the correct letter formation. Then in each duck they write a ‹qu› word and draw a picture for that word. Afterwards they colour the sheet. Colouring develops pencil control. Encourage the children to write and colour neatly.

Dictation: Read the words and sentences for the children to write down. The Dictation Master on page 171 may be photocopied onto the back of the spelling sheets for the children to write on.

Spelling list: Read the spelling words with the children. As a class, call out the sounds in the regular words, and say the letter names for the tricky words '**to**' and '**do**'. At the end of both these words, the letter ‹o› makes an /oo/ sound. The longer word 'squirrel' has two syllables and can be remembered as 'squir' and 'rel' for spelling. It helps the children remember the spelling if they emphasise the /e/ sound in the second syllable, pronouncing it to rhyme with 'bell'.

Dictation

1. quit
2. quick
3. quench
4. quail
5. quest
6. liquid

1. She is quick.
2. The ducks went quack.
3. The quiz was on Sunday.

Spelling List 5

1. on
2. but
3. **plum**
4. quick
5. quiz
6. queen
7. squid
8. **to**
9. **do**
10. squirrel

Write a ‹**qu**› word and draw a picture in each duck.

quack

qu

Action: Make a duck's beak with your hands and say *qu, qu, qu.*

Grammar 5 – Proper nouns

Prepare...
Story book
showing names
Grammar sheet 5
Black pencils
(Write up school
address)
(Atlases)

Aim: Develop the children's understanding that there are different types of words, and that each type has a special name.

Proper nouns are the names given to particular people and places, and to months and days of the week.

Introduction: The children practise saying the alphabet. Write or hold up capital letters and ask the children to say the name and/or sound for each. Ask some of the children to write their name on the board. Check that they have started their name with a capital letter. Ask the children what all the names on the board have in common. The answer is that they all start with a capital letter. Show the children some names in a story book. Point out that all the words start with a capital letter. Explain that people's names always start with a capital letter.

Main point: Special names that are given to people, places or things are called **Proper Nouns**. The children's names are proper nouns. They have a capital letter to show how important they are. Other names are special too and they also need a capital letter, e.g. the name of the school, road, town, county and country. The school address could be written out on a big piece of paper, or 'envelope', to be read with the children identifying the proper nouns. The proper nouns should all have capital letters. There is a page in the *Jolly Grammar Big Book 1* that will help introduce proper nouns.

Action: The action for a proper noun is to touch one's forehead with the index and middle fingers.

Colour: The colour for nouns is black. (If using a blackboard, explain that as there is no black chalk, white chalk is used instead.)

Grammar sheet 5: The children write in the outlined words Proper Nouns, using a black pencil. Then they draw a picture of themselves in the frame and write their name underneath, remembering to use a capital letter. There is a space for their surname as well. The children write the name of their teacher under the second frame, and draw a picture in it. Then they write the school address on the picture of the envelope.

Extension activity: The children write the names of others at their table, or in their class. They could look for the names of towns and countries in their atlases.

Rounding off: Call out words, some of which are proper nouns. For those that are proper nouns, the children do the action. For those that are not, they keep still.

Proper Nouns

Black

me

my teacher

Action: Touch forehead with index and middle fingers.

Colour: Black

Spelling 6 – ‹ar›

Prepare...
Flash cards:
• basic sounds
• tricky words
Spelling sheet 6
Spelling list 6
Star shape

Revision: Revise some basic sounds. Revise tricky words 'I', 'the', 'he', 'she', 'me', 'we', 'be', 'was', 'to' and 'do'.

Main point: Revise the ‹ar› spelling of the /ar/ sound. With the children, make a list of words which use it. Then ask them to make up sentences, using some of the words. The words could also be written onto a big star shape, which might then be used as a word bank for display. In some regions the letter ‹a› is also pronounced as /ar/, in words such as 'class', 'path' and 'father'. It may be helpful to make a list of these words, and to learn them by using the 'Say as it sounds' spelling technique.

Spelling sheet 6: The children write inside the outlined ar, using the correct letter formation. Then in each star they write an ‹ar› word and draw a picture for that word. Afterwards they colour the sheet. Colouring develops pencil control. Encourage the children to colour and write neatly.

Dictation: Read the words and sentences for the children to write down. Tell the children that the /k/ sound at the end of 'park' and 'shark' is a kicking ‹k›. Later they will learn rules to help them choose between ‹c›, ‹k› and ‹ck›. The Dictation Master on page 171 may be photocopied onto the back of the spelling sheets for the children to write on.

Spelling list: Read the spelling words with the children. As a class, call out the sounds in the regular words, and say the letter names for the tricky words **'are'** and **'all'**. Point out to the children that 'are' is only tricky because they must remember to put the ‹e› on the end. The longer word 'farmyard' has two syllables and can be remembered as 'farm' and 'yard' for spelling.

Dictation	
1. car	4. start
2. jar	5. shark
3. part	6. march

1. She has a red car.
2. I ran to the park.
3. A shark has sharp teeth.

Spelling List 6
1. at
2. yes
3. **slug**
4. arm
5. hard
6. scarf
7. card
8. **are**
9. **all**
10. farmyard

Write an ‹**ar**› word and draw a picture in each star.

Action: Open mouth wide and say *ah*, as if at the doctors.

Grammar 6 – Common nouns

Prepare...
Pictures of common nouns
Grammar sheet 6
Black pencils
(Camera)
(Jolly Grammar Big Book 1)

Aim: Develop the children's understanding of common nouns.

Introduction: Revise proper nouns with the class. Call out some words. For those that are proper nouns, the children do the action. Remind them that proper nouns need a capital letter at the beginning because they are important names.

Main point: Tell the children that not all names are important. The word 'chair' is a noun but it is not a proper noun. There are many chairs, not just one chair. These sorts of nouns are **Common Nouns**, and do not need capital letters. If it makes sense to put 'a', 'an' (the indefinite articles) or 'the' (the definite article) in front of a word, then the word is probably a noun. It may help the children's understanding to tell them that nouns are things that can be photographed. However, this is true only of concrete nouns, and not of abstract nouns such as 'happiness'. There is a page in the *Jolly Grammar Big Book 1* that will help introduce common nouns.

Action: The action for a common noun is to touch one's forehead with all the fingers of one hand.

Colour: The colour for nouns is black. (If using a blackboard, explain that as there is no black chalk, white chalk is used instead.)

Call out some words. The children do the action for those that are common nouns.

Grammar sheet 6: The children write inside the outlined words Common Nouns using a black pencil. Then, in each 'photograph', the children draw an object or animal. It may help them to look around and choose three things that they can see. The children write the common noun for each picture underneath it. In the next exercise, they read the sentences and write a noun that makes sense in each space. Then they draw pictures for their nouns in the 'photograph' frames.

Extension activity: The children write nouns and draw pictures for other things they can see around them. They can pretend they have a camera and look around for things to photograph.

Rounding off: Call out words including some proper nouns and some common nouns. For those that are proper or common nouns, the children do the appropriate action. For words that are neither they keep still.

Common Nouns

Black

Draw 3 pictures and write the nouns underneath.

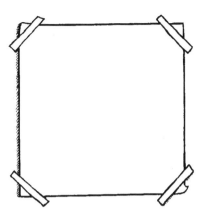 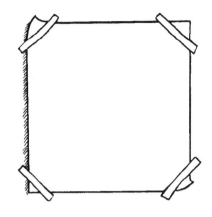 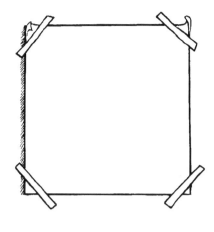

_____   _____   _____

Write a noun to finish each sentence, and draw a picture.

1. The _____ is black.

2. I throw the _____ .

3. A _____ can swim.

4. I like to eat _____ .

Action: Put hand on forehead.

Colour: Black

Spelling 7 – short vowels

Prepare...
Flash cards:
• basic sounds
• tricky words
Spelling sheet 7
Spelling list 7
(CVC word cards)
(Containers)

Revision: Revise some basic sounds. Revise tricky words 'he', 'she', 'me', 'we', 'be', 'was', 'to', 'do', 'are' and 'all'.

Main point: Revise the short vowels: /a/, /e/, /i/, /o/, /u/. The children could use their fingers to help them remember. They point to their thumb for /a/, their index finger for /e/, etc. Many spelling rules relate to the short vowels, so children need to be able to identify them in words.

Set out five containers, a bag, net, bin, box and mug, as on the sheet. Call out a word with a short vowel and ask the children to decide which short vowel sound is in the word, i.e. /a/ words go in the bag. /e/ words go in the net, etc. You could use the double page in the Grammar Big Book 1 and stick the words on it. (Also look at p17 for ideas on teaching short vowels.)

Spelling sheet 7: Call out CVC words for the children to write into the appropriate container. Alternatively you could put a selection of consonant/vowel/consonant word or picture cards on each table. The children look at them, and then write the words in the sppropriate containers. Ensure that there are at least three words for each vowel sound.

Dictation: Read the words and sentences for the children to write down. The Dictation Master on page 171 may be photocopied onto the back of the spelling sheets for the children to write on.

Spelling list: Read the spelling words with the children. This week's list is different, as it features most of the days of the week. As a class, say the letter names for the tricky words '**you**' and '**your**'. The longer two words 'Wednesday' and 'Saturday' have 3 syllables and can be remembered as 'Sat-ur-day' and 'Wed-nes-day'. Emphasise the /ue/ in 'Tuesday', and tell them that the /er/ sounds in 'Thursday' and 'Saturday' are both spelt <ur>.

Dictation	
1. Sunday	4. Wednesday
2. Monday	5. Thursday
3. Tuesday	6. week

1. It is Monday.
2. Yesterday was Sunday.
3. I swim on Thursdays.

Spelling List 7

1. dog
2. **bran**
3. Monday
4. Tuesday
5. Wednesday
6. Thursday
7. Friday
8. **you**
9. **your**
10. Saturday

Short Vowel Sounds

Think of some words for each short vowel sound and write them in the right container.

Aa   Ee   Ii   Oo   Uu

Grammar 7 – Alphabetical order

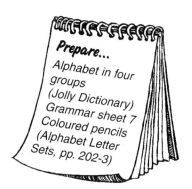

Prepare...
Alphabet in four groups
(Jolly Dictionary)
Grammar sheet 7
Coloured pencils
(Alphabet Letter Sets, pp. 202-3)

Aim: Develop the children's knowledge of the alphabet.

Introduction: The children need to be thoroughly familiar with each letter's position in the alphabet and dictionary. This will improve their ability to find words in the dictionary. Show the children a dictionary and explain what it is for. Tell the children that if a dictionary were divided into four approximately-equal parts, the letters would fall into the following groups:

1. Aa Bb Cc Dd Ee
2. Ff Gg Hh Ii Jj Kk Ll Mm
3. Nn Oo Pp Qq Rr Ss
4. Tt Uu Vv Ww Xx Yy Zz

The children practise saying the alphabet in these groups. They hold up one finger as they say the first group, pause, then hold up two fingers as they say the second, etc. A copy of the alphabet divided into the four groups should be available for them to see. There is a copy in the *Jolly Grammar Big Book 1,* and the four groups are incorporated in the *Jolly Dictionary.*

Main point: Point to, or hold up letters (both capital and lower-case), and ask for their names and/or sounds. Ask which letter comes after the one being shown, and which comes before it. This activity is ideal for any spare moments, and needs to be repeated often for the children to learn the alphabet thoroughly.

Grammar sheet 7: Using a different coloured pencil for each group, the children write inside the outlined lower-case letters. Then they write the capital letters next to the lower-case ones. Next they write the letters that come before and after those in each group of books. Finally they try putting groups of letters into alphabetical order. The letters in each group of three are consecutive, and should be written as capitals.

Extension activity: Put more letters on the board, or letter cards on tables, for the children to put into alphabetical order.

Rounding off: Give each child a different letter from one of the Alphabet Letter Sets on pages 202-3. Call out a letter. The child with that letter stands up. Then ask who has the letter that comes after it, and who has the letter that comes before. The children stand next to each other holding their letters in front of them.

Alphabetical Order

Use a different colour for each section of the alphabet.
Write the capital letters next to the lower-case letters.

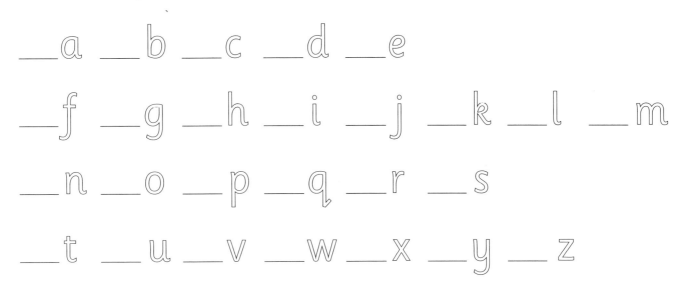

__a __b __c __d __e

__f __g __h __i __j __k __l __m

__n __o __p __q __r __s

__t __u __v __w __x __y __z

Which letters come before and after?

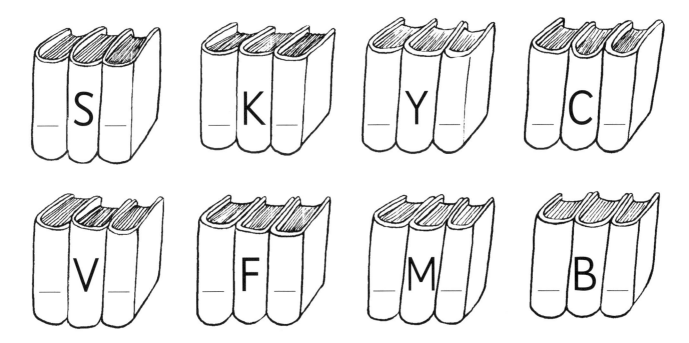

Put these sets of letters into alphabetical order.

C A B

__ __ __

M L K

__ __ __

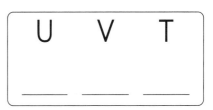

U V T

__ __ __

Spelling 8 – ‹ff›

Prepare...
Flash cards:
• single letters
• tricky words
Spelling sheet 8
Spelling list 8
Cliff shape

Revision: Revise some basic sounds. Revise tricky words 'me', 'we', 'be', 'was', 'to', 'do', 'are', 'all', 'you' and 'your'.

Main point: Introduce the ‹ff› spelling of the /f/ sound. An ‹f› at the end of a small word, with a short vowel, is usually doubled, except for the words 'if' and 'of'. Explain to the children that they can remember the difference between 'of' and 'off' by listening to the sound at the end of the word. If it is a /f/ sound, as in 'off', then they must use ‹ff›, but if they hear a /v/ sound, as in 'of', they only need one ‹f›. With the children, make a list of words which use ‹ff›. Then ask them to put the words into sentences. The words could also be written onto a big cliff shape.

Spelling sheet 8: The children write inside the outlined *ff*. Then in each cliff they write an ‹ff› word and draw a picture to go with it. Afterwards they colour the sheet.

Dictation: Read the words and sentences for the children to write down. The Dictation Master on page 171 may be photocopied onto the back of the spelling sheets for the children to write on.

Spelling list: Read the spelling words with the children. Go over the tricky words **'come'** and **'some'**. The longer word 'stuffing' has two syllables and can be remembered as 'stuff' and 'ing' for spelling.

Dictation

1. off
2. cuff
3. huff
4. gruff
5. ruff
6. cliff

1. He can jump off the step.
2. She ran up the cliff.
3. We must not sniff.

Spelling List 8

1. up
2. man
3. **cr**ab
4. off
5. cliff
6. stiff
7. cuff
8. **come**
9. **some**
10. stuffing

Write an ‹ff› word and draw a picture on each cliff.

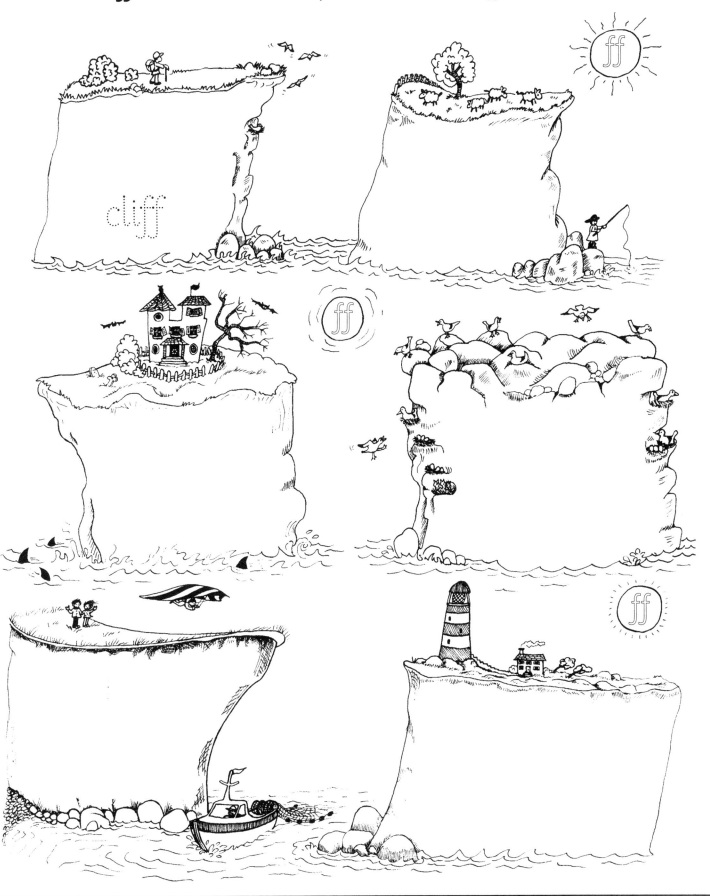

 Action: Let hands gently come together as if fish deflating and say
f f f f f f.

Prepare...
Write up examples
Grammar sheet 8
(Mouse puppet
and box)

Grammar 8 – 'a' or 'an'

Aim: Develop the children's knowledge of when to use the 'an' instead of 'a'. ('A' and 'an' are the indefinite articles.

Introduction: Revise the five vowel letters. Tell the children that all the other letters are called consonants. Revise the short vowel sounds /a/, /e/, /i/, /o/, /u/.

Use a box and puppet to help them listen for the short vowel sounds:
For /a/, put the puppet **at** the side of the box. For /e/, make the puppet wobble on the **e**dge of the box. For /i/, put the puppet **in** the box. For /o/, put the puppet **on** the box. For /u/, put the puppet **u**nder the box.

The chidren can make a fist with one hand. They pretend that this is the box and that their other hand is Inky Mouse. Call out the short vowel sounds, or words with a short vowel in, and the children do the appropriate action. (See pictures on page 17).

Main point: Write the following sentences on the board, and read them in turn with the class. Ask the children to help identify, and underline, the nouns. Ask what is wrong with the sentences and correct them.

> 'An shark has an fin.'
> 'They saw a elephant at the zoo.'

Explain that in general, if a noun starts with a vowel sound we use 'an', and if it starts with a consonant we use 'a'. If it makes sense to put 'a', 'an' or the definite article 'the' in front of a word, then the word is probably a noun. Call out nouns, some of which begin with a vowel, for the children to decide whether to use 'a' or 'an'.

Grammar sheet 8: Go over the sheet with the children, asking what each picture shows. If necessary, sound out and write the words on the board. The children can either just write 'a' or 'an' underneath each picture, or they can write the noun for the picture as well.

Extension activity: The children write down as many nouns as they can think of which begin with a vowel. They could use a dictionary to help them.

Rounding off: Go over the sheet with the class. Then ask each child for a word beginning with a vowel.

a or an ?

Write 'an' before each word beginning with a vowel, and 'a' for the others.

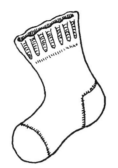

_____

_____

_____

_____

_____

_____

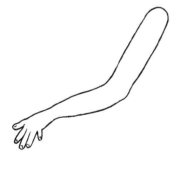

_____

_____

_____

Aa   Ee   Ii   Oo   Uu

Spelling 9 – ‹ll›

Revision: Revise some basic sounds. Revise tricky words **'be'**, **'was'**, **'to'**, **'do'**, **'are'**, **'all'**, **'you'**, **'your'**, **'come'** and **'some'**.

Main point: Introduce the ‹ll› spelling of the /l/ sound. An ‹l›, at the end of a small word with a short vowel, is usually doubled. With the children, make a list of words which use ‹ll›. Then ask them to put the words into sentences. The words could also be written onto a big bell shape.

Spelling sheet 9: The children write inside the outlined ll. Then in each bell they write an ‹ll› word and draw a picture to go with it. Afterwards they colour the sheet.

Dictation: Read the words and sentences for the children to write down. The Dictation Master on page 171 may be photocopied onto the back of the spelling sheets for the children to write on.

Spelling list: Read the spelling words with the children. Go over the tricky words **'said'** and **'here'**. The longer word 'windmill' has two syllables and can be remembered as 'wind' and 'mill' for spelling.

Dictation

1. ill   4. doll
2. tell   5. smell
3. gull   6. drill

1. You must tell your Mum.
2. She fell ill.
3. He can spell well.

Spelling List 9

1. red
2. win
3. **drum**
4. will
5. bell
6. doll
7. skull
8. **said**
9. **here**
10. windmill

Write an ‹ll› word and draw a picture in each bell.

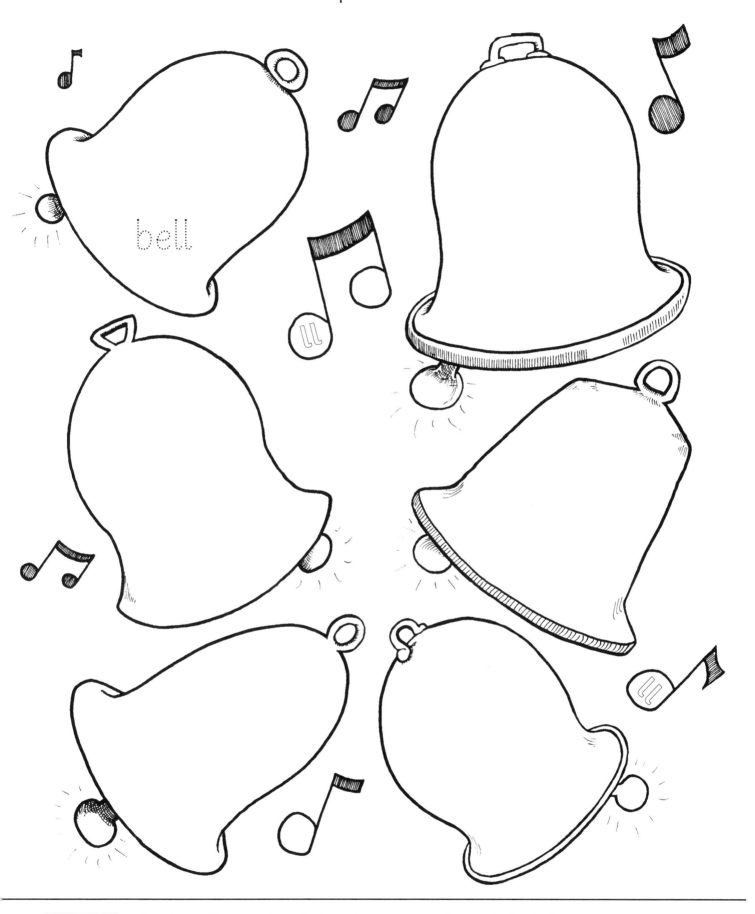

 Action: Pretend to lick a lollipop and say l, l, l, l.

Prepare...
Picture showing
several of same
thing.
Grammar sheet 9
('Pull-Out Plurals',
p. 209)

Grammar 9 – Plurals

Aim: Develop the children's understanding of singular and plural, and their knowledge that the simplest way to make the plural of a word is to add ‹s›.

Introduction: Hide any copies of the alphabet. Sit the children in a circle, and ask one child to say the first letter of the alphabet. Go round the circle, with each child saying the next letter. Repeat this, choosing a different child to start each time, so that they do not always say the same letter.

Main point: Hold up a picture of a dog and ask the children what it shows. Then hold up a picture of several dogs, and ask what this picture shows. Write 'dog' and 'dogs' on the board. Ask the children how the two words differ. Explain that nouns usually change when they describe more than one. The name for nouns which describe one of something is **singular**, and the name for nouns which describe more than one is **plural**. The simplest way of making a plural is by adding an ‹s› to the end of the noun. Call out examples of singular nouns and ask the children to give plurals for them, e.g. for 'one cat' they say 'lots of cat**s**'. Only call out nouns which have regular plurals.

Examples:

cat	rat	flag	hen	ant	pig	tree
bird	bun	bed	drum	pen	map	leg
doll	van	cloud	duck	bat	car	boat

Grammar sheet 9: The children read each noun and decide whether it is singular or plural. They draw a picture for each, remembering that for plural nouns they must draw more than one item. Then they look at the pictures in the boxes underneath. They write the noun for each picture, remembering that if it shows more than one item, they must add an ‹s› to make the plural.

Extension activity: The children could do the 'Pull-Out Plurals' Sheet on page 209.

Rounding off: Go over the sheet with the class, checking which nouns are plural and which singular.

Plurals

Draw a picture for each word.

hats · · · · · · · · · pens · · · · · · · · · dog

cars · · · · · · · · · cow · · · · · · · · · frog

Write the word for each picture.

_____   _____   _____

_____   _____   _____

Spelling 10 – ‹ss› / ‹zz›

Prepare...
Flash cards:
• basic sounds
• new spellings
• tricky words
Spelling sheet 10
Spelling list 10
Dress shape

Revision: Revise some basic sounds and ‹ff›. Revise tricky words 'to', 'do', 'are', 'all', 'you', 'your', 'come', 'some', 'said' and 'here'.

Main point: Introduce the ‹ss› spelling of the /s/ sound, and the ‹zz› spelling of the /z/ sound. A /s/ or /z/ at the end of a small word, with a short vowel, is usually doubled. There are very few words with the ‹zz› spelling, which is why it is included here with ‹ss›. With the children, make a list of words which use ‹ss› and ‹zz›. Then ask them to put the words into sentences. The words could also be written onto a big dress shape, with a bee shape drawn on it for the ‹zz› words.

Spelling sheet 10: The children write inside the outlined ss and zz. Then they write an ‹ss› word in each dress, and a ‹zz› word in the bee, and draw a picture for each word. Afterwards they colour the sheet.

Dictation: Read the words and sentences for the children to write down. The Dictation Master on page 66 may be photocopied onto the back of the spelling sheets for the children to write on.

Spelling list: Read the spelling words with the children. Go over the tricky words 'there' and 'they'. For the word 'there', ask the children to look for the word 'here' within it. The longer word 'crossroad' has two syllables and can be remembered as 'cross' and 'road' for spelling.

Dictation

1. hiss
2. buzz
3. fuss
4. jazz
5. cross
6. press

1. She was cross with him.
2. You must press the bell.
3. I will miss you.

Spelling List 10

1. ox
2. run
3. **from**
4. buzz
5. cross
6. less
7. miss
8. **there**
9. **they**
10. crossroad

Write an ‹**ss**› word in each dress and a ‹**zz**› word in the bee.
Draw a picture for each word.

dress

 Action: Weave hand in an s shape, like a snake, and say *sssssss.*

 Action: Put arms out at sides and pretend to be a bee saying *zzzzzzzzzz.*

Grammar 10 – Pronouns

Aim: Develop the children's knowledge of personal pronouns.

Introduction: Tell the children a story without using any pronouns.

Example: 'Peter was having a birthday party. Peter wanted to blow up some balloons. Peter blew too hard and burst one of the balloons. Peter's sister laughed. Peter's sister helped Peter to blow up some more balloons.'

Ask the children why the story sounds wrong.

Main point: Tell the children that to avoid continually repeating names, we use other, short words to take their place. These short words are called **pronouns**. Pronouns take the place of nouns. Check that the children remember what a noun is. Tell the children the main pronouns. There is an action for each one:

Actions:

I	–	point to self
you	–	point to someone else
he	–	point to a boy
she	–	point to a girl
it	–	point to the floor
we	–	point in a circle to include self and others
you	–	point to two other people
they	–	point to the next-door class

Colour: The colour for pronouns is pink.

Tell the children that the words 'we' and 'they' are plural. The word 'you' appears twice. Make sure the children understand that it is singular the first time and plural the second. This will help them when they begin to learn other languages.

Grammar sheet 10: The children write inside the outlined word, Pronouns, in pink. Then they write inside the other outlined pronoun words in pink. They read the pronouns and draw pictures for them. For 'I', they draw themselves. If the pronoun is plural they must draw more than one person.

Extension activity: The children could write a sentence for each pronoun. The Writing Master on page 172 may be photocopied onto the back of the grammar sheets for the children to write on.

Rounding off: Go over the actions with the class.

Pronouns  *Pink*

Colour the pronouns pink. Draw a picture for each pronoun.
Remember which are singular and which are plural.

Spelling 11 – ‹ck›

Prepare...
Flash cards:
• basic sounds
• new spellings
• tricky words
Spelling sheet 11
Spelling list 11
Chick shape

Revision: Revise some basic sounds and the spellings covered so far. Revise tricky words 'are', 'all', 'you', 'your', 'come', 'some', 'said', 'here', 'there' and 'they'.

Main point: Revise the ‹ck› spelling of the /c/ sound. At the end of a small word with a short vowel, a /c/ sound is usually doubled by adding a kicking ‹k›. With the children, make a list of words which use ‹ck›. Then ask them to put the words into sentences. The words could also be written onto a big chick shape.

Spelling sheet 11: The children write inside the outlined ck. Then in each chick they should write a ‹ck› word and draw a picture to go with it. Afterwards they colour the sheet.

Dictation: Read the words and sentences for the children to write down. The Dictation Master on page 171 may be photocopied onto the back of the spelling sheets for the children to write on.

Spelling list: Read the spelling words with the children. Go over the tricky words 'go' and 'no', reminding the children that if a word sounds wrong with a short vowel sound they should try saying it with the vowel's name instead. The longer word 'broomstick' has two syllables and can be remembered as 'broom' and 'stick' for spelling.

Dictation

1. pack
2. luck
3. peck
4. brick
5. block
6. truck

1. Pack your bag.
2. The boys had a quick snack.
3. This will bring you luck.

Spelling List 11

1. hop
2. fit
3. **grin**
4. duck
5. neck
6. clock
7. lick
8. **go**
9. **no**
10. broomstick

Write a ‹**ck**› word and draw a picture in each chick.

 Action: Raise hand and snap fingers as if playing castanets and say
ck, ck, ck.

Grammar 11 – Initial blends wheel

Prepare...
Flash cards
• consonant blends
Grammar sheet 11
Scissors
Split pins
(Cardboard/glue)
(Extra paper)

Aim: Develop the children's awareness of initial consonant blends for reading and writing.

Introduction: Children will read words with consonant blends more easily if they are familiar with them, and blend them almost automatically, e.g. '/dr/-/u/-/m/' rather than '/d/-/r/-/u/-/m/'. The individual consonant sounds are not always easy to hear in blends, so knowing them also helps with writing. Call out examples of words containing initial consonant blends, and ask the children to sound them out. Often the children will sound them out using the blend. Ask how they would write the blend sound. Ask them to hold up one finger for each sound.

Examples:	flag	press	slip	stop	drum
	clap	glen	crib	frog	slug
	glad	green	swim	prod	club

Main point: Use the Consonant Blends Flash Cards on pages 181-85 to practise reading consonant blends with the class. First hold up the cards and ask the children to say the sound the blend makes, eg. /fr/, /gl/, /sm/. Then go through the cards again, saying each blend for the children without letting them see the card. Ask them to say the two sounds that make up each blend. They should count each sound on their fingers.

Grammar sheet 11: The children cut out the two discs. The smaller disc is placed on top of the larger one and a split pin is used to fasten them together. They can be strengthened if they are glued onto card or thick paper before being pinned together. The children turn the discs around and blend the letters to see how many words they can make.

Extension activity: The children write a list of all the words they have found.

Rounding off: Go round the class, asking each child for one of their words. Hopefully there will be plenty of different ones.

Initial Blends Wheel

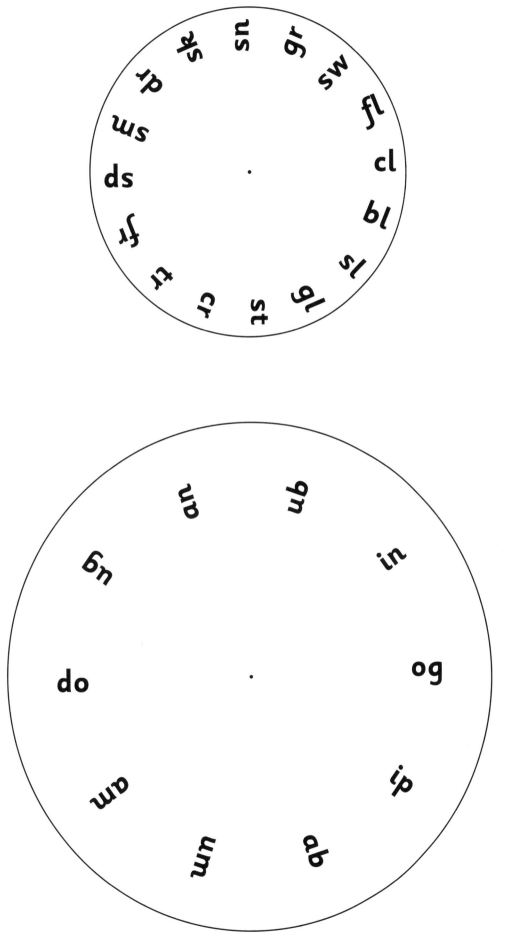

Spelling 12 – ‹y› at end

Prepare...
Flash cards:
• basic sounds
• new spellings
• tricky words
Spelling sheet 12
Spelling list 12
Holly shape

Revision: Revise some basic sounds and the other spellings covered so far. Revise tricky words 'you', 'your', 'come', 'some', 'said', 'here', 'there', 'they', 'go' and 'no'.

Main point: Remind the children that the main way of writing the /ee/ sound is <ee>. But when there is an /ee/ sound at the end of a multi-syllabic word it is usually written with a <y>. The letter <y> only makes a /y/ sound when it comes at the beginning of a word. The rest of the time it is replacing the letter <i> (shy i) as in cherry/cherries. However it is usually pronounced as an /ee/ sound. It often comes after double letters as it is taking the place of the vowel <i> and so is counted as a vowel. If the consonants are not doubled it will still change the sound of the vowel preceding it (see page 17). With the children, make a list of words that end with a <y> making an /ee/ sound. The words could also be written on a large holly leaf shape, which can then be used as a word bank for display.

Spelling sheet 12: The children write inside the outlined y. Then in each holly leaf they write a word that ends with <y> and draw a picture for that word. Afterwards they colour the sheet.

Dictation: Read the words and sentences for the children to write down. The Dictation Master on page 171 may be photocopied onto the back of the spelling sheets for the children to write on.

Spelling list: Read the spelling words with the children. As a class, call out the sounds in the regular words, and say the letter names for the tricky words 'so' and 'my'. For 'so', remind the children that if a word sounds wrong with a short vowel sound they should try saying it with the long vowel sound instead. In 'my' the <y> is again taking the place of (shy) <i>, but this time it is making the /ie/ sound. The longer word 'family' has 3 syllables and can be remembered as 'fam-i-ly' for spelling.

Dictation	
1. silly	4. fluffy
2. fuzzy	5. mucky
3. sleepy	6. frosty

1. It was a very funny story.
2. Sally has a dressing up party.
3. The car was rusty and mucky.

Spelling List 12
1. bed
2. wet
3. **prod**
4. holly
5. party
6. story
7. happy
8. **so**
9. **my**
10. family

Write a word with ‹y› at the end and draw a picture in each holly leaf.

holly

 Action: Put hands on head as if ears on a donkey and say *ee*. (This comes from the *ee or* action.)

Spelling sheet 12

Grammar 12 – Initial blends

Prepare...
Alphabet in four groups
Flash cards
• consonant blends
Grammar sheet 12 (Initial blends wheel)

Aim: Develop the children's awareness of initial consonant blends for reading and writing.

Introduction: Help the children practise saying the alphabet in the four groups. There should be a copy available for them to see. Ask them to find the vowels. Then ask what all the other letters are called. Hold up flash cards with consonant blends for the children to read.

Main point: Call out some consonant blends (see Grammar 11) and ask the children to say which sounds they would need to spell them. They should hold up one finger for each sound they say. Ask tthem for examples of words starting with each of the blends.

Grammar sheet 12: Go over the sheet with the children and ask them what each picture shows. The first six pictures use words that are on their 'initial blends wheels'. The words for the other six pictures are not on the wheels, but the children can use the blends on the inner disc to help them.

(Answers:
grin	frog	drum
crab	skip	slug
flag	tree	star
snail	swing	spoon)

Extension activity: Write some initial consonant blends on the board, e.g. ‹fl›, ‹sl›, ‹gr›, and ask the children to think of, or find, as many words as possible beginning with each blend.

Rounding off: Go over the sheet with the class, sounding out each word.

Initial Blends

Write the word for each picture.

Use your initial blends wheel to help you.

g r i n

_ _ _ _

_ _ _ _

_ _ _ _

_ _ _ _

_ _ _ _ _

These words are not on your wheel but you can use the initial blends on the inner wheel to help you.

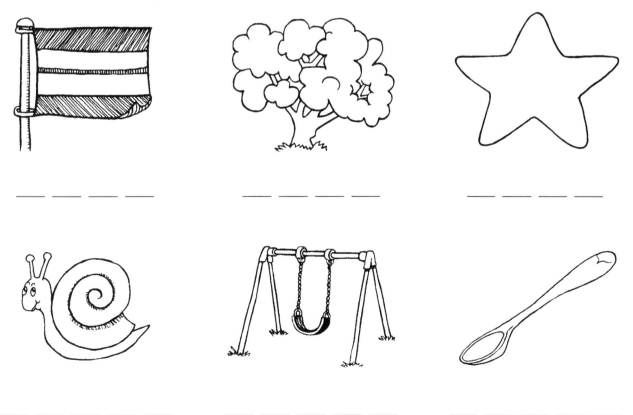

_ _ _ _

_ _ _ _

_ _ _ _

_ _ _ _ _

_ _ _ _ _

_ _ _ _ _

Spelling 13 – **vowels**

Revision: Revise some basic sounds and the other spellings covered so far. Revise tricky words '**come**', '**some**', '**said**', '**here**', '**there**', '**they**', '**go**', '**no**', '**so**' and '**my**'.

Main point: Revise the short vowel sounds /a/, /e/, /i/, /o/ and /u/. Vowel letters are different from consonants because they can use their names in words: /ai/, /ee/, /ie/, /oa/ and /ue/, – as well as their sounds. There are also other vowel sounds, besides the sounds and names of the five vowel letters. Digraphs with at least one vowel letter, e.g. ‹oi›, ‹ou›, ‹er› and ‹oo›, also make vowel sounds. Tell the children that all words in English must have at least one vowel sound. Call out some words. If a word contains a short vowel sound, the children do the action to show whether Inky is <u>a</u>t, on the <u>e</u>dge of, <u>i</u>n, <u>o</u>n or <u>u</u>nder the box (see picture on page 17). If not they put their hands in their laps.

Spelling sheet 13: The children read the words in the leaves. If a word has a short vowel sound they colour its edge yellow. When they have found all the short vowel words they could colour the remaining leaf edges green. (The colours can be altered to suit.)

When the children have completed the sheet, read through the words, with the class identifying which have short vowel sounds and which do not.

Dictation: Read the words and sentences for the children to write down. The Dictation Master on page 171 may be photocopied onto the back of the spelling sheets for the children to write on.

Spelling list: Read the spelling words with the children. As a class, say the letter names for the tricky words '**one**' and '**by**'. In 'by', the ‹y› is taking the place of (shy) ‹i›. Spellings 4-7 are colour words. Other colours are covered elsewhere in the spelling lists. The longer word 'colour' has two syllables and can be remembered as 'col' and 'our' for spelling.

Dictation	
1. pain	4. coat
2. deep	5. rescue
3. lie	6. coin

1. She sleeps in a bed.
2. We sat on the train.
3. The soap fell on the floor.

Spelling List 13
1. sad
2. let
3. **trip**
4. blue
5. orange
6. grey
7. black
8. **one**
9. **by**
10. colour

Vowels

Decide whether each word has a short vowel sound.
If it does, colour its leaf edge yellow.

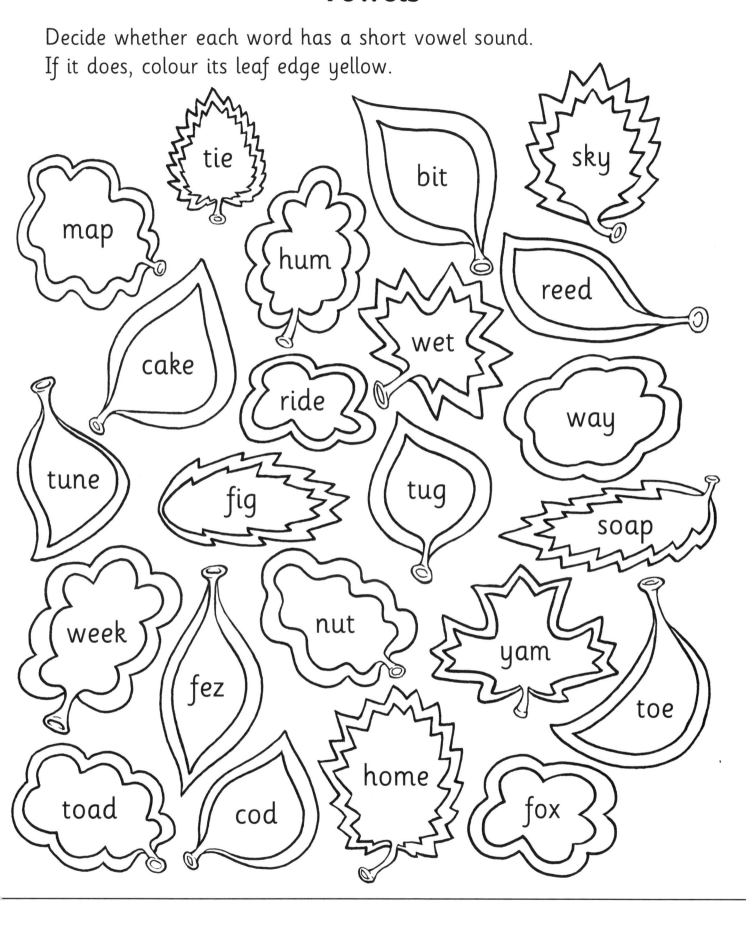

Aa Ee Ii Oo Uu

Grammar 13 – Alphabetical order

Prepare...
Alphabet in four groups
Dictionaries
Grammar sheet 13
Coloured pencils
(Alphabet Letter Sets, pp. 202-3)

Aim: Develop the children's knowledge of the alphabet, and their ability to use word books and dictionaries.

Introduction: The children practise saying the alphabet in the four groups. They hold up one finger as they say the first group, and pause, then hold up two fingers as they say the second, etc. A copy of the alphabet divided into the four groups should be available for them to see. Use the Alphabet Poster, or the alphabet in the *Jolly Gramar Big Book 1*. Call out letters. Ask the children which group each letter belongs to, e.g. 's' is in group 3. Show the children a dictionary. Explain again that the words are in alphabetical order to make them easier to find. Knowing where a letter falls in the alphabet will help the children decide where to look for it in the dictionary. Remind them that the colours on the edge of the pages of the *Jolly Dictionary* will help them do this.

Main point: Give out dictionaries for the children to look at, sharing if necessary. Call out a letter and ask the children to try finding words beginning with it in the dictionary. Repeat with other letters. This activity should be repeated often in any spare moments. Children need a lot of practice at finding the right place in the dictionary. Once they improve they can race each other to find letters.

Grammar sheet 13: Using a different coloured pencil for each group, the children write inside the outlined capital letters. Then they write the lower-case letters next to the capitals. In the next section there are letters for the children to find in the dictionary. They find the first word for each letter and write in on the sheet. Finally the children try putting groups of letters into alphabetical order. This time the letters in each group of three are not consecutive, and are lower-case rather than capital.

Extension activity: Let the children look through the dictionary, reading the meaning of words that interest them. Put more letters on the board, or letter cards on the tables, for the children to find in the dictionary.

Rounding off: Go over the sheet with the children. See which words they found, and put the sets of letters into alphabetical order.

Alphabetical Order

To find words in the dictionary, it helps to think of the alphabet in sections.
Use a different colour for each section of the alphabet (red, yellow, green, blue).
Write the lower-case letters next to the capital letters.

A_ B_ C_ D_ E_

F_ G_ H_ I_ J_ K_ L_ M_

N_ O_ P_ Q_ R_ S_

T_ U_ V_ W_ X_ Y_ Z_

Using a **Dictionary**

Dictionaries tell you how a word is spelt and what it means.
Find each letter in your dictionary and write down the first word it gives for that letter.

Aa _____   Gg _____

Ss _____   Nn _____

Oo _____   Zz _____

Put these sets of letters into alphabetical order.

e a c	k f m	n s q	z w v
__ __ __	__ __ __	__ __ __	__ __ __

Spelling 14 – ‹a_e›

Revision: Revise some basic sounds and the other spellings covered so far. Revise tricky words '**said**', '**here**', '**there**', '**they**', '**go**', '**no**', '**so**', '**my**', '**one**' and '**by**'.

Main point: Remind the children that the main ways of writing the /ai/ sound are ‹ai›, ‹a_e› and ‹ay›. Revise the ‹a_e› spelling of the /ai/ sound, which can be referred to as '‹a› hop-over ‹e›'. It is important for the children to understand that the ‹e› is a 'magic ‹e›'. Although it makes no sound in the word, the ‹e› sends magic over the consonant before it, to change the short vowel sound to a long one. With the children, make a list of words which use ‹a_e›. Then ask them to make up sentences, using some of the words. To see the difference 'magic ‹e›' makes, try covering it in some of the words and then reading them again, e.g. 'cape' becomes 'cap'. The words could also be written onto the shape of a big bunch of grapes.

Spelling sheet 14: In each grape, the children write ‹a_e› in the spaces. Then they read the words and draw pictures to go with them. Afterwards they colour the sheet.

Dictation: Read the words and sentences for the children to write down. The Dictation Master on page 171 may be photocopied onto the back of the spelling sheets for the children to write on.

Spelling list: Read the spelling words with the children. As a class, call out the sounds in the regular words, and say the letter names for the tricky words '**only**' and '**old**'. The children can learn both of these words by saying the letter names as they write them. The longer word 'pavement' has two syllables and can be remembered as 'pave' and 'ment' for spelling.

Dictation

1. mad	4. ate
2. made	5. scrap
3. at	6. scrape

1. Mum made a cake.
2. The gate is open.
3. She was late.

Spelling List 14

1. ran
2. hat
3. **scar**
4. came
5. grape
6. name
7. cake
8. **only**
9. **old**
10. pavement

Add ‹**a_e**› to make a word in each grape. Read the words and draw pictures for them.

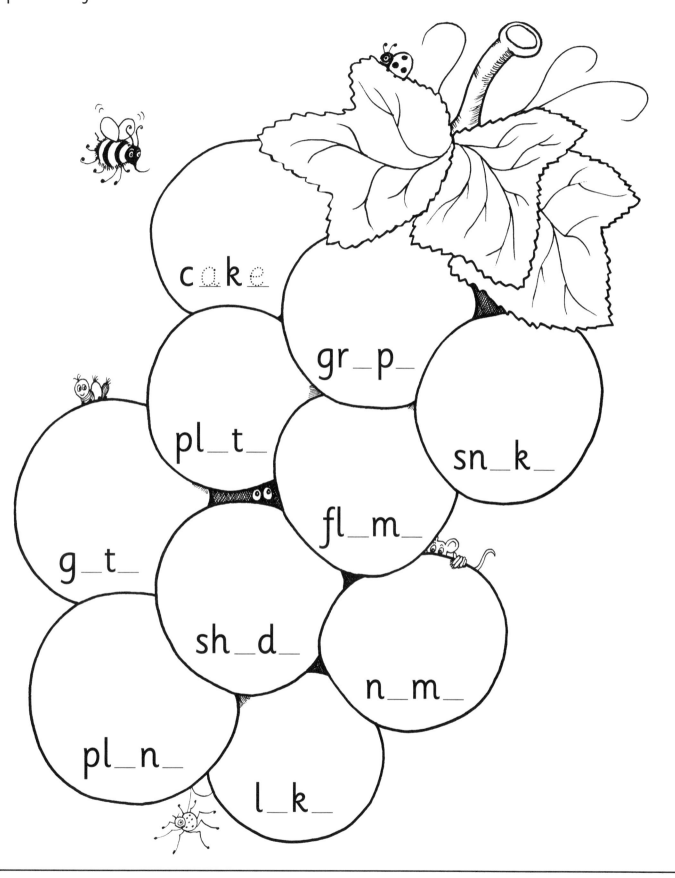

c a k e

gr_p_

pl_t_

sn_k_

g_t_

fl_m_

sh_d_

n_m_

pl_n_

l_k_

Action: Cup hand over ear and say *ai, ai, ai.*

Grammar 14 – Verbs

Prepare...
Write up examples
Action picture
Grammar sheet 14
Red pencils
('Verb Bee', p 212)
(Drawing paper)

Aim: Develop the children's knowledge of verbs.

Introduction: Revise the parts of speech covered so far: proper and common nouns, and pronouns. Call out some nouns for the children to do the appropriate actions. As a class, say the pronouns with their actions. Write some sentences on the board.

Examples: The bees play football. Bill kicks the ball. He scores a goal.

With the children, find the nouns and pronouns , and underline the words in the correct colour, using black or, if necessary, white for nouns, and pink for pronouns.

Main point: Tell the children that another type of word is a **verb**. For young childen a verb can be defined as a 'doing' word.

Action   The action for verbs is to clench fists and move arms backwards and forwards at sides, as if running.

Colour: The colour for verbs is red.

Look at a picture showing lots of things happening. There is a page for verbs in the *Jolly Grammar Big Book 1* showing bees busy doing lots of different things. With the children, make a list of verbs for the actions in the picture. Generally children will say the verbs in gerund form, e.g. 'skipping'. Teach them that this is part of the verb 'to skip'. Write the infinitive 'to skip' on the board. The root word in this instance is 'skip'. Verb roots change according to the tense, to show when they take place.

Grammar sheet 14: Help the children name the verbs for the bees' actions in the first three pictures. The children complete the infinitives by writing the verb roots, and should not add ‹-ing›. Read the next three words with the class. The children draw a bee doing each of these actions. Finally the children think of three verbs themselves and complete the infinitives in the spaces. Then they draw a bee doing each of these actions.

Extension activity: Using the 'Verb Bees' template on page 212, the children draw big 'verb bees'. They each choose one of the verbs, and draw on the template to show their bee doing the action for it, adding legs, wings, etc. They carefully colour in their bees. The 'verb bees' can used to make a verb wall display.

Rounding off: Ask the children which verbs they wrote. Call out words, including proper nouns, common nouns and verbs. The children do the appropriate action for each word.

 **Red**

Busy Bees

Write the verb for each picture.

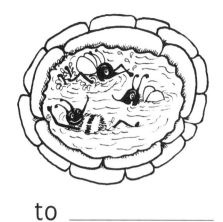

to _____   to _____   to _____

Draw a Bee doing each verb.

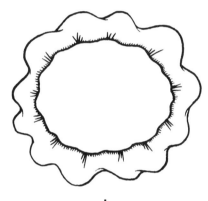

to cry   to hop   to brush

Think of 3 more verbs.

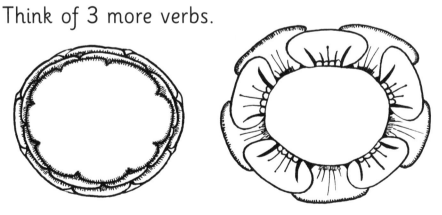

to _____   to _____   to _____

Action: Move arms backwards and forwards at sides as if running.

Colour: Red

Spelling 15 – ‹i_e›

Revision: Revise some basic sounds and the other spellings covered so far. Revise tricky words 'there', 'they', 'go', 'no', 'so', 'my', 'one', 'by', 'only' and 'old'.

Main point: Remind the children that the main ways of writing the /ie/ sound are ‹ie›, ‹i_e›, ‹igh› and ‹y›. Revise the ‹i_e› spelling of the /ie/ sound, which can be referred to as '‹i› hop-over ‹e›'. It is important for the children to understand that the ‹e› is a 'magic ‹e›'. Although it makes no sound in the word, the ‹e› sends magic over the consonant before it, to change the short vowel sound to a long one. With the children, make a list of words which use ‹i_e›. Then ask them to make up sentences, using some of the words. To see the difference 'magic ‹e›' makes, try covering it in some of the words and then reading them again, e.g. 'ride' becomes 'rid'. The words could also be written onto a big kite shape.

Spelling sheet 15: In each kite, the children write ‹i_e› in the spaces. Then they read the words and draw pictures to go with them. Afterwards they colour the sheet.

Dictation: Read the words and sentences for the children to write down. The Dictation Master on page 171 may be photocopied onto the back of the spelling sheets for the children to write on.

Spelling list: Read the spelling words with the children. As a class, call out the sounds in the regular words, and say the letter names for the tricky words 'like' and 'have'. 'Like' is not really a tricky word, but the children must remember that the /ie/ sound is made with the ‹i_e› spelling. Point out to the children that 'have' is only tricky because they must remember to put an ‹e› at the end. The ‹e› is there because English words do not end in ‹v›. The longer word 'bridesmaid' has two syllables and can be remembered as 'brides' and 'maid' for spelling.

Dictation	
1. wine	4. slide
2. win	5. spine
3. slid	6. spin

1. I like my prize.
2. She has a red bike.
3. They had a kite.

Spelling List 15
1. six
2. pad
3. **smell**
4. bike
5. time
6. smile
7. prize
8. **like**
9. **have**
10. bridesmaid

Add ‹**i_e**› to make a word in each kite. Read the words and draw pictures for them.

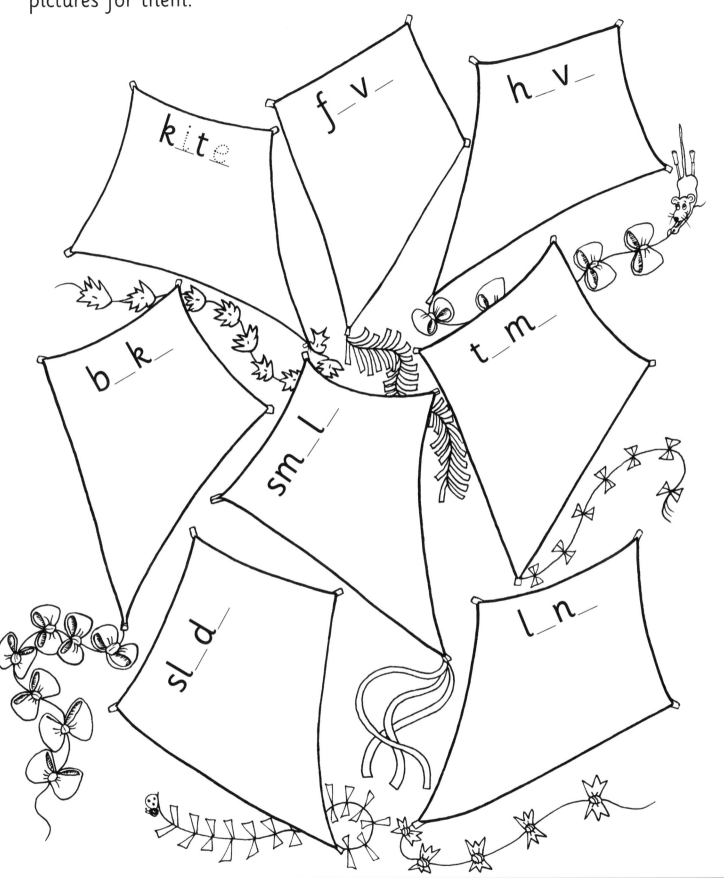

k_i_t_e

f_v_

h_v_

b_k_

t_m_

sm_l_

sl_d_

l_n_

 Action: Stand to attention and salute saying *ie, ie.*

Grammar 15 – Conjugating Verbs

Prepare...
Write up example
Grammar sheet 15
Pencils
• red
• pink

Aim: Develop the children's knowledge of verbs.

Introduction: Revise verbs. Call out words, including proper nouns, common nouns and verbs, for the children to do the appropriate actions. N.B. Many common verbs can also be nouns, e.g. 'to smile' or 'a smile'. For the purposes of this lesson, try to use only those verbs which cannot also be nouns.

Examples of verbs which cannot be used as nouns:

to eat	to clean	to see	to fill	to draw	to live
to make	to give	to hear	to sew	to wear	to bring

Write some sentences on the board. With the children, find the proper nouns, common nouns, pronouns and verbs, and underline them in the correct colours.

Example: 'Mum drives a car. We help Mum clean it.'

Main point: Revise pronouns and their actions (see Grammar 10). Now choose a verb, e.g. 'to eat', and tell the class that they are going to join it to the pronouns. With the children, say:

I eat,	you eat,	he eats,	she eats,	it eats,
we eat,	you eat,	they eat.		

This is called **conjugating** a verb. Tell the children that for he, she and it, (the third person singular), they must add an ‹s› to the verb root. Ask the children to think of some more verbs, and conjugate them with the appropriate actions for the pronouns and verbs.

Grammar sheet 15: The children write inside the outlined word, Verbs, in red. Then either choose a verb as a class, or let each child choose a different one. The children write their verb on the line provided at the top of the sheet, and use a pink pencil to write inside the outlined pronouns. Then they write their verb beside each pronoun. Remind the children that for 'he', 'she' and 'it', an ‹s› must be added to the verb root. Also remind them that 'I', 'you', 'he','she' and 'it' are singular, and that 'we', 'you' and 'they' are plural. The children draw a picture to show the person or people doing the action for their verb.

Extension activity: Ask the children to think of other verbs and conjugate them.

Rounding off: Do the action for a pronoun, and then mime a verb. See if the children can work out what you are 'saying', e.g. Point to a girl and pretend to write something; the children answer 'She writes'.

Verbs  *Red*

Think of a verb and write it on the line.

to_____

Draw a picture for each person doing the verb.
Remember the 3rd person needs an 's' added at the end, and that for a plural you must draw more than one person.

1st person singular	2nd person singular	3rd person singular

I _____   you _____   he
she _____
it

1st person plural	2nd person plural	3rd person plural

we _____   you _____   they _____

Spelling 16 – ‹o_e›

Prepare...
Flash cards:
• basic sounds
• new spellings
• tricky words
Spelling sheet 16
Spelling list 16
Tadpole shape

Revision: Revise some basic sounds and the other spellings covered so far. Revise tricky words **'go'**, **'no'**, **'so'**, **'my'**, **'one'**, **'by'**, **'only'**, **'old'**, **'like'** and **'have'**.

Main point: Remind the children that the main ways of writing the /oa/ sound are ‹oa›, ‹o_e› and ‹ow›. Revise the ‹o_e› spelling of the /oa/ sound, which can be referred to as '‹o› hop-over ‹e›'. It is important for the children to understand that the ‹e› is a 'magic ‹e›'. Although it makes no sound in the word, the ‹e› sends magic over the consonant before it, to change the short vowel sound to a long one. With the children, make a list of words which use ‹o_e›. Then ask them to make up sentences, using some of the words. To see the difference 'magic ‹e›' makes, try covering it in some of the words and then reading them again, e.g. 'hope' becomes 'hop'. The words could also be written onto a big tadpole shape.

Spelling sheet 16: In each tadpole, the children write ‹o_e› in the spaces. Then they read the words and draw pictures to go with them. Afterwards they colour the sheet.

Dictation: Read the words and sentences for the children to write down. The Dictation Master on page 171 may be photocopied onto the back of the spelling sheets for the children to write on.

Spelling list: Read the spelling words with the children. As a class, call out the sounds in the regular words, and say the letter names for the tricky words **'live'** and **'give'**. Tell the children to be particularly careful with 'live', as it could take either an /ie/ sound or a short /i/ sound. When reading, they will have to work out which word is meant from the context. Again, despite the ‹i_e› spelling, 'give' has an /i/ sound. The ‹e› is there because English words do not end in ‹v›. The longer word 'tadpole' has two syllables and can be remembered as 'tad' and 'pole' for spelling.

Dictation

1. rode	4. hop
2. rod	5. note
3. hope	6. not

1. Time to go home.
2. Those roses are pink.
3. The mole is in his hole.

Spelling List 16

1. cod
2. lot
3. **sn**ap
4. bone
5. nose
6. home
7. globe
8. **live**
9. **give**
10. tadpole

Add ‹**o_e**› to make a word in each tadpole. Read the words and draw pictures for them.

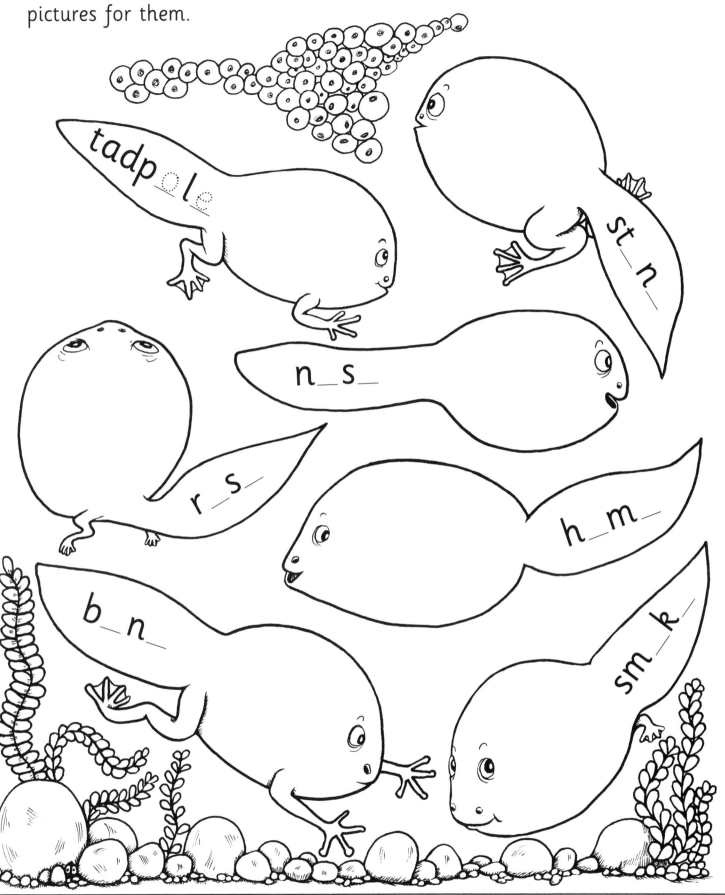

 Action: Bring hand over mouth as if something terrible has happened and say *oh!*

Prepare...
Write up examples
Grammar sheet 16
Pencils
• black
• red

Grammar 16 – Past Tense

Aim: Develop the children's knowledge of the past tense. Explain that the simple past tense of a regular verb is formed by adding ‹ed› to the root.

Introduction: Call out words, including proper and common nouns, pronouns and verbs, for the children to do the appropriate actions. When calling out a word that can function as either a verb or a noun, e.g. 'to smile' or 'a smile', see which action the children do. Explain that both are right, as the word can be either a verb or a noun. The children enjoy doing both actions at once, with one hand touching their forehead while the other 'runs' at their side. Ask the children how they would know whether a word was a noun or a verb if they read it in a sentence. Write two sentences on the board, e.g. for the word 'race':

Examples: 'She races up the hill.' (verb)   'She runs in a race.' (noun)

With the children, look at the words in the sentences. Decide which parts of speech they are, and underline them in the appropriate colours. It is important that the children realise that a word can function as more than one part of speech, and that they need to look at the context to see how it is being used.

Main point: Explain that verbs often change to show when the action takes place. So far the verbs taught have all been in the **present tense**, which means they describe actions taking place now. If, however, the verb describes an action which has already taken place, it should be in the **past tens**e. So, 'Today I wish' is in the present and 'Yesterday I wished' is in the past. The past tense of a regular verb is made by adding the suffix ‹ed› to the root. If the root ends with an ‹e›, the children should remove it before adding ‹ed›. The ‹ed› can make three different sounds, either /id/ as in 'hated', /d/ as in 'saved', or /t/ as in 'missed'.

Actions: The action for the present tense is pointing towards the floor with the palm of the hand.
The action for the past tense is pointing backwards over the shoulder with a thumb.

Colour: The colour for verbs is red.

Call out verbs in the present and past tenses for the children to do the actions.

Grammar sheet 16: With the children, read through the sheet. The children write the verbs in the past tense. Then they decide if the sentences are in the present or past tenses.

Extension activity: Put some sentences on the board in the present tense and ask the children to write the sentences in the past tense on the back of their sheet.

Rounding off: With the children, go through the sheet and any additional work.

Past Tense

The simplest way to make the past tense is by adding ‹**ed**› to the verb.

Today I talk	talk + ed	**Yesterday I talked**

If a verb already ends with an ‹**e**›, cross it off and then add ‹**ed**›.

Today I smile	smile + ed	**Yesterday I smiled**

Put these words into the past tense.

Present	Past	Present	Past
jump	_____	hope	_____
paint	_____	play	_____
like	_____	wave	_____
shout	_____	skate	_____

Underline the verbs in red.
Then decide if these sentences are in the present or past.

She brushed her hair.	(past) / present
They look out of the window.	past / present
I cooked dinner.	past / present
The race started in the park.	past / present

 Action (Past): Point thumb backwards over shoulder.

Spelling 17 – ‹u_e›

Prepare...
Flash cards:
• basic sounds
• new spellings
• tricky words
Spelling sheet 17
Spelling list 17
'Tune' note shape

Revision: Revise some basic sounds and the other spellings covered so far. Revise tricky words '**so**', '**my**', '**one**', '**by**', '**only**', '**old**', '**like**', '**have**', '**live**' and '**give**'.

Main point: Remind the children that the main ways of writing the /ue/ sound are ‹ue›, ‹u_e› and ‹ew›. Revise the ‹**u_e**› spelling of the /ue/ sound, which can be referred to as '‹u› hop-over ‹e›'. It is important for the children to understand that the ‹e› is a 'magic ‹e›'. Although it makes no sound in the word, the ‹e› sends magic over the consonant before it, to change the short vowel sound to a long one. With the children, make a list of words which use ‹u_e›. Then ask them to make up sentences, using some of the words.. To see the difference 'magic ‹e›' makes, try covering it in some of the words and then reading them again, e.g. 'use' becomes 'us'. The ‹u_e› is a difficult spelling because it sometimes makes an /oo/ sound, as in 'rude'. The words could also be written onto a big 'tune' note shape.

Spelling sheet 17: In each note of the tune, the children write ‹u_e› in the spaces. Then they read the words and draw pictures to go with them. Afterwards they colour the sheet.

Dictation: Read the words and sentences for the children to write down. The Dictation Master on page 171 may be photocopied onto the back of the spelling sheets for the children to write on.

Spelling list: Read the spelling words with the children. As a class, call out the sounds in the regular words, and say the letter names for the tricky words '**little**' and '**down**'. The longer word 'useless' has two syllables and can be remembered as 'use' and 'less' for spelling.

Dictation

1. us
2. use
3. cub
4. cube
5. tube
6. tub

1. She has a tube of sweets.
2. Soon we will see the duke.
3. The girl played a tune.

Spelling List 17

1. bus
2. pot
3. **sw**im
4. cube
5. tune
6. used
7. excuse
8. **little**
9. **down**
10. useless

Add ‹**u_e**› to make a word in each note of the tune. Read the words and draw pictures for them.

c u b e

m _ l _

t _ b _

t _ n _

d _ k _

Action: Point to people around you and say *you, you, you.*

Prepare...
Grammar sheet 17
Red pencils

Grammar 17 – Doubling Rule

Aim: Develop the children's ability to recognise the short vowels in words, so that they learn when to apply the doubling rule before adding ‹-ed›.

Introduction: With the children, say the alphabet in the four groups. See if the children can do this without reading it. Revise the vowels. Revise present and past tenses. Call out verbs in the present and past tenses for the children to do the actions (see Grammar 16).

Main point: Tell the children that endings that are added to words are called **suffixes**. If a word has a short vowel sound, it is important to be careful when adding a suffix that starts with a vowel, such as ‹-ed›. This is because the ‹e› behaves like a magic ‹e›, and changes the vowel sound in the word. For example, if ‹-ed› is added to 'hop' it becomes 'hoped'. The short /o/ sound becomes a long /oa/, which completely changes the meaning of the word. To avoid this we use the **doubling rule**. The consonant at the end of the root word is doubled to make a 'wall'. The magic from the ‹e› cannot jump over a wall of more than one letter. (See picture on page 18.) The children are unlikely to remember this rule immediately, but will gradually do so through revisiting and applying it.

Examples of verb roots needing the doubling rule:

> fit   slip   skip   clap   grab

If the children ask about a word like 'stamped', explain that it already has a wall made by the two consonants ‹m› and ‹p›. Words that do not have short vowel sounds, e.g. 'look', 'play' and 'bark', do not need a wall, and so do not need to double the last consonant.

Grammar sheet 17: The children write the verb roots in the past tense, remembering to apply the doubling rule.

Extension activity: Ask the children to draw a picture of the 'magic' from the ‹e› being unable to cross a thick 'wall' of two consonants.

Rounding off: Call out some verbs. The children listen for the vowel sounds. For verbs which have a short vowel sound, they do the actions for Inky and the box (see picture on page 17). For verbs that do not, the children put their hands in their laps.

Past Tense

Write these verbs in the simple past tense.

bat _____

hop _____

pat _____

rip _____

nod _____

peg _____

hug _____

wag _____

hum _____

Spelling 18 – ‹wh›

Revision: Revise some basic sounds and the other spellings covered so far. Revise tricky words **'one'**, **'by'**, **'like'**, **'have'**, **'live'**, **'give'**, **'only'**, **'old'**, **'little'** and **'down'**.

Main point: Revise the ‹wh› spelling of the /w/ sound. With the children, make a list of words which use it, or give them some examples. Then ask them to make up sentences, using some of the words. The words could also be written onto a big whale shape.

Spelling sheet 18: The children write inside the outlined wh. Then in each whale they write a ‹wh› word and draw a picture to go with it. Afterwards they colour the sheet.

Dictation: Read the words and sentences for the children to write down. The Dictation Master on page 171 may be photocopied onto the back of the spelling sheets for the children to write on.

Spelling list: Read the spelling words with the children. As a class, call out the sounds in the regular words, and say the letter names for the tricky words **'what'** and **'when'**. Tell the children that the question words 'what', 'where', 'when', 'why', 'who' and 'which' are all ‹wh› words. Other question words will be covered in later spelling lists. The longer word 'whenever' has three syllables. It can be remembered as the two shorter words 'when' and 'ever' for spelling.

Dictation

1. when
2. whisk
3. whizz
4. which
5. whale
6. whisker

1. My cat is black and white.
2. The rabbit has long whiskers.
3. What did you whisper?

Spelling List 18

1. did
2. cut
3. **twin**
4. whale
5. wheel
6. white
7. whisper
8. **what**
9. **when**
10. whenever

Write a ‹**wh**› word and draw a picture in each whale.

whale

wh

wh

Action: Blow on to open hand, as if you are the wind, and say *wh, wh, wh.*

Grammar 18 – The Future

Prepare...
Grammar sheet 18
Red pencils

Aim: Develop the children's understanding of verbs, so they know that a verb can describe the past, present or future.

Introduction: Revise present and past tenses with the children. Call out verbs in the present and past tenses for the children to do the appropriate actions (see Grammar 16). Call out some verbs in the present tense. Make a point of choosing verbs which have a regular simple past tense, such as 'to cook', 'to hop' or 'to race'. Ask the children to put these verbs into the past. Then call out some verbs in the past tense and ask the children to put them into the present.

Main point: When a verb describes an action taking place in the future, the verb root does not take a suffix, as in the past tense. Instead it has an extra word put in front of it. The extra word is another verb, called an auxiliary verb. The auxilliary verb used to describe the future is the verb 'to be'. 'Shall' is added for the first person, ('I' and 'we'), and 'will' for the second and third persons. (The verb 'to be' is competely irregular, but is essential. The future of the verb 'to be' is 'I shall, you will, he/she/it will, we shall, you will, they will'.)

Example of a verb in the future: 'to jump':

I shall jump,	you will jump	he will jump,	she will jump
it will jump	we shall jump,	you will jump	they will jump.

Actions: The action for verbs which describe the future is pointing to the front.

Colour: The colour for verbs is red.

Call out some verbs and ask the children to put them into the future.

Grammar sheet 19: The children write the verbs in the past tense in the 'Yesterday' column, and in the future in the 'Tomorrow' column. Then they write some sentences about what they did yesterday and what they will do tomorrow.

Extension activity: Ask the children to write some more sentences about what they did yesterday. The Writing Master on page 172 may be photocopied onto the back of the grammar sheets for the children to write on.

Rounding off: With the children, choose a verb and conjugate it in the past, present and future.

Future

Past Yesterday		Future Tomorrow
I _____	I cook	I ____ _____
I _____	I listen	I ____ _____
I _____	I skate	I ____ _____
I _____	I walk	I ____ _____

Write some sentences about what you did yesterday.

_____

_____

_____

Write some sentences about what you will do tomorrow.

_____

_____

_____

A sentence must have a verb.
Underline the verbs in your sentences in red.

 Action (Future): Point to the front.

Spelling 19 – ‹ay›

Prepare...
Flash cards:
• basic sounds
• new spellings
• tricky words
Spelling sheet 19
Spelling list 19
Crayon shape

Revision: Revise some basic sounds and the other spellings covered so far. Revise tricky words 'only', 'old', 'like', 'have', 'live', 'give', 'little', 'down', 'what' and 'when'.

Main point: Remind the children that the main ways of writing the /ai/ sound are ‹ai›, ‹a_e› and ‹ay›. Revise the ‹ay› spelling of the /ai/ sound. Tell the children that the ‹ay› spelling is often used at the end of words. The ‹y› takes the place of (shy) ‹i›, since the letter ‹i› does not like to be at the end of words. Then ask them to make up sentences, using some of the words. The words could also be written onto a big crayon shape.

Spelling sheet 19: The children write inside the outlined ay. Then in each crayon they write an ‹ay› word and draw a picture for that word. Afterwards they colour the sheet.

Dictation: Read the words and sentences for the children to write down. The Dictation Master on page 171 may be photocopied onto the back of the spelling sheets for the children to write on.

Spelling list: Read the spelling words with the children. As a class, call out the sounds in the regular words, and say the letter names for the tricky words 'why' and 'where'. Tell the children that the question words 'what', 'when', 'why', 'who', 'where' and 'which' are all ‹wh› words (see Spelling 18, pages 94-5). The longer word 'playground' has two syllables, and can be remembered as 'play' and 'ground' for spelling.

Dictation

1. hay
2. way
3. play
4. tray
5. clay
6. Sunday

1. You can all stay here.
2. Today is hot.
3. I made this from clay.

Spelling List 19

1. an
2. cat
3. **sk**in
4. say
5. away
6. play
7. today
8. **why**
9. **where**
10. playground

Write an ‹**ay**› word and draw a picture in each crayon.

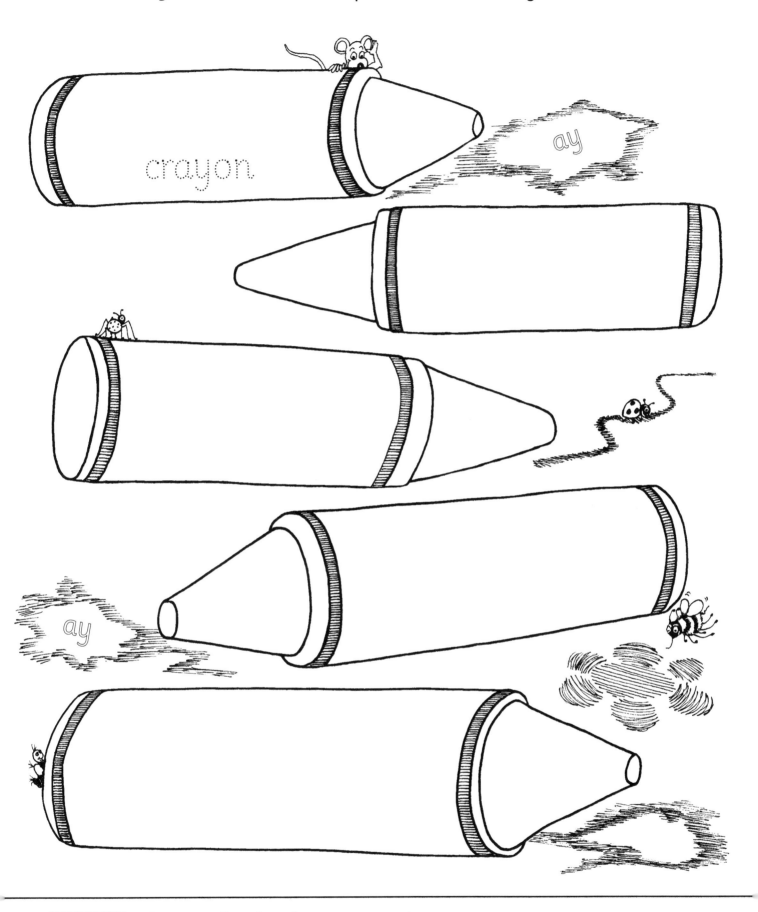

crayon

ay

ay

Action: Cup hand over ear and say *ai, ai, ai.*

Grammar 19 – Alphabetical order

Prepare...
Alphabet in four groups
Write up examples
Grammar sheet 19
Coloured pencils
Dictionaries

Aim: Develop the children's knowledge of the alphabet, and their ability to use word books and dictionaries.

Introduction: The children sit in a circle, and one child says the first letter of the alphabet. Going round the circle, each child says the next letter. Then the children practise saying the alphabet in the four groups. They hold up one finger as they say the first group, and pause, then hold up two fingers as they say the second, etc. Call out letters. Ask the children which group each letter belongs to, e.g. 's' is in group 3. Knowing where a letter falls in the alphabet will help the children work out where to look for it in the dictionary.

Main point: Look at a copy of the dictionary. Explain that the words are listed in alphabetical order to make them easier to find. Words can be arranged in alphabetical order just as letters can. Write some words on the board. To avoid confusion at this stage, make sure each word begins with a different letter. The children look at the first letter of each word to help them arrange the words in alphabetical order.

Grammar sheet 19: Using a different coloured pencil for each group, the children write inside the outlined lower-case letters. The first group should be red, the next yellow, then green and the last blue. Then they write the capitals next to the lower-case letters. In the next section the children put groups of letters into alphabetical order. Then they try putting groups of words into alphabetical order.

Extension activity: Give out dictionaries for the children to look at, sharing if necessary. Write some letters on the board. Ask the children to find words beginning with these letters in the dictionary. The Writing Master on page 172 may be photocopied onto the back of the grammar sheets for the children to write on. If the children are able, they could also copy out the words' meanings.

Rounding off: Go over the sheet, with the children putting the words into alphabetical order. Call out letters and see if the children can find the right section for them in the dictionary.

Alphabetical Order

Use a different colour for each section of the alphabet. The first should be red, then yellow, then green and the last blue.
Write the capital letters next to the lower-case letters.

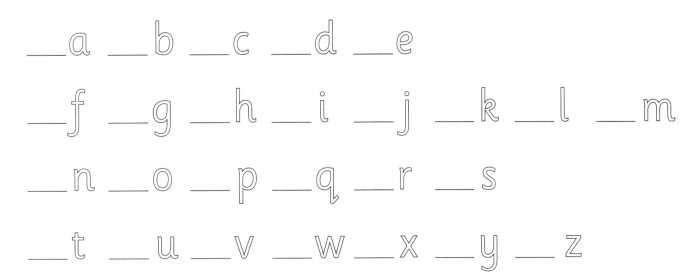

__a __b __c __d __e
__f __g __h __i __j __k __l __m
__n __o __p __q __r __s
__t __u __v __w __x __y __z

Put these sets of letters into alphabetical order.

F B X O	T C N H	q w i r
___ ___ ___ ___	___ ___ ___ ___	___ ___ ___ ___

Put these words into alphabetical order.

Inky   Snake   Bee

_____   _____   _____

pear   apple   orange

_____   _____   _____

Spelling 20 – ‹ea›

Prepare...
Flash cards:
• basic sounds
• new spellings
• tricky words
Spelling sheet 20
Spelling list 20
Teapot shape

Revision: Revise some basic sounds and the other spellings covered so far. Revise tricky words '**like**', '**have**', '**live**', '**give**', '**little**', '**down**', '**what**', '**when**', '**why**' and '**where**'.

Main point: Remind the children that the main ways of writing the /ee/ sound are ‹ee› and ‹ea›. Revise the ‹**ea**› spelling of the /ee/ sound. With the children, make a list of words which use it. Then ask them to make up sentences, using some of the words. The words could also be written onto a big teapot shape.

Spelling sheet 20: The children write inside the outlined ea. Then in each teapot they write an ‹ea› word and draw a picture to go with it. Afterwards they colour the sheet.

Dictation: Read the words and sentences for the children to write down. The Dictation Master on page 171 may be photocopied onto the back of the spelling sheets for the children to write on.

Spelling list: Read the spelling words with the children. As a class, call out the sounds in the regular words, and say the letter names for the tricky words '**who**' and '**which**'. Tell the children that the question words 'what', 'where', 'when', 'why', 'who' and 'which' are all ‹wh› words (see Spelling 18, pages 94-5). The longer word 'seaside' has two syllables and can be remembered as 'sea' and 'side' for spelling.

Dictation

1. sea	4. clean
2. peas	5. leaf
3. meat	6. teapot

1. They had beans for tea.
2. She took the dog on the beach.
3. He has peas in his garden.

Spelling List 20

1. met
2. web
3. **spin**
4. tea
5. heat
6. leaf
7. each
8. **who**
9. **which**
10. seaside

Write an ‹**ea**› word and draw a picture in each teapot.

ea

teapot

ea

Action: Put hands on head as if ears on a donkey and say *ee*. (This comes from the *ee or* action.)

Prepare...
Write up examples
Grammar sheet 20
Black pencils
(Dictionaries)

Grammar 20 – Nouns

Aim: Develop the children's understanding of nouns, and their ability to identify nouns in sentences.

Introduction: Revise the parts of speech covered so far: proper and common nouns, pronouns and verbs. Call out words for the children to do the appropriate actions. Remember that some words can function as both nouns and verbs, so the children can do both actions.

Main point: Look at the picture on Grammar sheet 20. Ask the children to give examples of nouns. Remind them that we can put 'a' (the indefinite article) or 'the' (the definite article) before those that are common nouns. Write some sentences on the board. Go through the sentences, finding the proper and common nouns with the children.

Examples: 'The farmer drives a tractor.'
              'My dog goes to the vet on Monday.'

Underline the nouns in black. If using a blackboard, explain that as there is no black chalk, white chalk is used instead.

Grammar sheet 20: The children look at the picture and write six nouns for things they can see. Remind them about when to use the indefinite articles 'a' and 'an' (see Grammar 8). Then the children read the sentences underneath and underline the nouns in black. Tell them that there can be more than one noun in a sentence.

Extension activity: The children write some sentences about the picture and underline the nouns. The Writing Master on page 172 may be photocopied onto the back of the grammar sheets for the children to write on. The children could also look up their six nouns in the dictionary.

Rounding off: Go over the sheet, with the children identifying the nouns.

Nouns

 Black

Write 6 nouns for what you can see in the picture.

a _____   the _____

a _____   the _____

a _____   the _____

Underline the nouns in these sentences in black.
There can be more than one noun in a sentence.

1. The cat is black and white.

2. Jim drives a red tractor.

3. The sheep are on the hills.

4. On Andrew's farm, there are cows, horses, sheep, pigs and chickens.

Spelling 21 – ‹igh›

Revision: Revise some basic sounds and the other spellings covered so far. Revise tricky words **'live'**, **'give'**, **'little'**, **'down'**, **'what'**, **'when'**, **'why'**, **'where'**, **'who'** and **'which'**.

Main point: Remind the children that the main ways of writing the /ie/ sound are ‹ie›, ‹i_e›, ‹igh› and ‹y›. Revise the **‹igh›** spelling of the /ie/ sound. With the children, make a list of words which use it. Then ask them to make up sentences, using some of the words. The words could also be written onto a big light-bulb shape.

Spelling sheet 21: The children write inside the outlined igh. Then in each light bulb they write an ‹igh› word and draw a picture to go with it. Afterwards they colour the sheet.

Dictation: Read the words and sentences for the children to write down. The Dictation Master on page 171 may be photocopied onto the back of the spelling sheets for the children to write on.

Spelling list: Read the spelling words with the children. As a class, call out the sounds in the regular words, and say the letter names for the tricky words **'any'** and **'many'**. The longer word 'frightening' has three syllables and can be remembered as 'frigh', 'ten' and 'ing', for spelling It helps the children remember the spelling if they emphasise the /e/ sound in the second syllable, pronouncing it to rhyme with 'pen'.

Dictation	
1. high	4. sight
2. sigh	5. bright
3. thigh	6. flight

1. It was a dark night.
2. My dad had a fright.
3. There was a bright light.

Spelling List 21

1. lip
2. his
3. **went**
4. night
5. high
6. might
7. light
8. **any**
9. **many**
10. frightening

Write an ‹**igh**› word and draw a picture in each light bulb.

Action: Stand to attention and salute saying *ie, ie.*

Grammar 21 – Adjectives

Prepare...
Snake picture
Write up sentence
Grammar sheet 21
Blue pencils
Coloured pencils
('Adjective Snake',
p. 213)

Aim: Develop the children's understanding of adjectives. Adjectives are words which describe nouns.

Introduction: Ask each child for an example of a common noun, e.g. 'a dog', 'a hat'.

Main point: Find, or draw, a picture of some snakes. If drawing the snakes, colour them in. Ask the children what the picture shows, and which part of speech the word 'snake' is (i.e. a noun). Write the following sentence on the board:

Sentence: This is a snake.

Underline the noun. Tell the children that this sentence does not tell us very much about the snake. Look at the adjective page in the *Jolly Grammar Big Book 1*, and choose one of the snakes in the picture. Ask the children for words to describe the snake, which could be added to the sentence to make it more interesting, e.g. 'long', 'green', 'spotty', 'sad', 'old'. Choose one of the describing words and add it to the sentence on the board. Tell the children that a word which describes a noun is called an **adjective**.

Action: The action for an adjective is to touch the side of the temple with a fist.

Colour: The colour for adjectives is blue.

Underline the adjective in your sentence in blue, while the children do the action. Choose some more snakes from the picture and ask for adjectives to describe them. Choose one of the snakes and, with the children, find as many adjectives to describe it as possible.

Grammar sheet 21: The children read the adjectives in the speech bubbles. Then they colour each snake to make it fit its adjective. The 'long' snake needs to have his 'long' body added. The children complete the phrase at the bottom of the sheet by writing three more adjectives which might describe a snake. Then they colour the snake underneath to fit these adjectives.

Extension activity: The photocopiable master on page 215 shows a section of a snake's body. The children each choose an adjective and colour their section of the snake accordingly. The sections can then be stuck together, with a head and tail added (see pages 214 and 216), to make 'Adjective Snakes'. The snakes can have any number of middle sections. The finished snake can be used for display.

Rounding off: With the children, look at any finished 'adjective snakes' and say the phrase 'a _____ , _____ , _____ snake', filling in the blanks with appropriate adjectives.

Colour the snakes to make them fit the adjectives.

You can use more than one adjective at a time.
Colour this snake to make it fit your description.

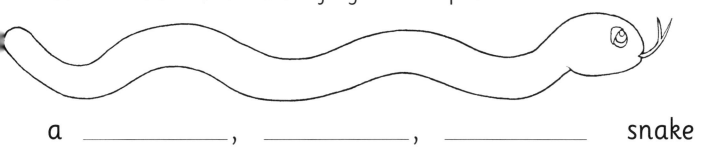

a _____ , _____ , _____ snake

 Action: Touch side of temple with fist.

Spelling 22 – ‹y›

Prepare...
Flash cards:
• basic sounds
• new spellings
• tricky words
Spelling sheet 22
Spelling list 22
Frying-pan shape

Revision: Revise some basic sounds and the other spellings covered so far. Revise tricky words 'little', 'down', 'what', 'when', 'why', 'where', 'who', 'which', 'any' and 'many'.

Main point: Remind the children that the main ways of writing the /ie/ sound are ‹ie›, ‹i_e›, ‹igh› and ‹y›. Revise the ‹y› spelling of the /ie/ sound. With the children, make a list of words which use it. Then ask them to make up sentences, using some of the words. The words could also be written onto a big frying-pan shape.

Spelling sheet 22: The children write inside the outlined y. Then in each frying pan they write a ‹y› word and draw a picture for that word. Afterwards they colour the sheet.

Dictation: Read the words and sentences for the children to write down. The Dictation Master on page 171 may be photocopied onto the back of the spelling sheets for the children to write on.

Spelling list: Read the spelling words with the children. As a class, call out the sounds in the regular words, and say the letter names for the tricky words 'more' and 'before'. The longer word 'myself' has two syllables and can be remembered as 'my' and 'self' for spelling.

Dictation

1. my
2. dry
3. sty
4. crying
5. flying
6. trying

1. Pigs live in a sty.
2. They are flying with me.
3. He was trying to sing the song.

Spelling List 22

1. win
2. sit
3. **stop**
4. fry
5. dry
6. crying
7. sky
8. **more**
9. **before**
10. myself

Write a ‹**y**› word and draw a picture in each frying pan.

Grammar 22 – Adjectives

Prepare...
Grammar sheet 22
Pencils
• black
• blue
(Jolly Grammar
Big Book 1)

Aim: Develop the children's ability to identify nouns and adjectives in sentences.

Introduction: Revise common nouns. Choose a noun, e.g. 'a horse'. Ask one child to say the noun with an adjective to describe it, e.g. 'a big horse'. Ask each child in turn to repeat what has been said and to add a new adjective, as in a memory game, e.g. 'a big, brown horse', 'a big, brown, kind horse', etc.

Main point: Revise adjectives. Think of some nouns, e.g. 'chair', 'jumper', 'dog', 'sandwich' etc. Ask the children for an adjective to go with each noun. Use one of their suggestions to make a simple sentence, and write it on the board, e.g. 'He had a little dog.' Underline the noun in black and the adjective in blue.

Grammar sheet 22: The children read the adjectives in the snake. Then they read the sentences in the middle of the sheet. They choose one of the adjectives for each sentence, and write it in the space. The adjectives can be used more than once.

Extension activity: The children underline the nouns in black and the adjectives in blue.

Rounding off: Go over the sheet with the children, seeing which adjectives they have chosen for each sentence. As long as their adjectives make sense in the sentences, the children's answers are right.

Adjectives  *Blue*

Find an adjective to describe each noun.
There are some adjectives in the snake to help you.
Underline the nouns in black.

A _____ snake hisses.

My _____ shirt is new.

The _____ dog barks.

Her _____ car stopped.

The sky is _____.

The tree is _____.

The _____ flowers smell.

The film was _____.

His _____ balloon burst.

My _____ coat is warm.

red
striped
green
long
yellow
pretty
blue
tall
pink
small
spotty

Spelling 23 – ‹ow›

Prepare...
Flash cards:
• basic sounds
• new spellings
• tricky words
Spelling sheet 23
Spelling list 23
Snowman shape

Revision: Revise some basic sounds and the other spellings covered so far. Revise tricky words '**what**', '**when**', '**why**', '**where**', '**who**', '**which**', '**any**', '**many**', '**more**' and '**before**'.

Main point: Remind the children that the main ways of writing the /oa/ sound are ‹oa›, ‹o_e› and ‹ow›. Revise the ‹**ow**› spelling of the /oa/ sound. With the children, make a list of words which use it. Then ask them to make up sentences, using some of the words. The words could also be written onto a big snowman shape.

Spelling sheet 23: The children write inside the outlined ow. Then in each snowman they write an ‹ow› word, and draw a picture to go with it. Afterwards they colour the sheet.

Dictation: Read the words and sentences for the children to write down. The Dictation Master on page 171 may be photocopied onto the back of the spelling sheets for the children to write on.

Spelling list: Read the spelling words with the children. As a class, call out the sounds in the regular words, and say the letter names for the tricky words '**other**' and '**were**'. For 'other', the children should use the 'Say as it Sounds' method, and pronounce the ‹o› in the first syllable to rhyme with 'bother'. For 'were', the children should say the names of the letters as they write them. The longer word 'snowman' has two syllables and can be remembered as 'snow' and 'man' for spelling.

Dictation

1. own
2. low
3. mow
4. show
5. grow
6. throw

1. It has started snowing.
2. The seeds have grown well.
3. There is a show on Monday.

Spelling List 23

1. box
2. job
3. bu**lb**
4. own
5. grow
6. elbow
7. yellow
8. **other**
9. **were**
10. snowman

Write an ‹**ow**› word and draw a picture in each snowman.

Grammar 23 – Final Blends

Prepare...
Flash cards
• initial blends
• final blends
Grammar sheet 23
Coloured pencils
(Unfinished word/
final blend cards)

Aim: Develop the children's ability to recognise final blends.

Introduction: Revise initial blends. Hold up flash cards of initial blends for the children to read. Then call out blends for the children to say which letters are in them.

Main point: Tell the children that not all blends come at the beginning of words. Some come at the end of words and are called final blends. Hold up some flash cards of final blends and ask the children to blend them. On the board, write an example of a word using each blend. Call out some of the final blends and ask the children which letter sounds are in them.

Examples:	lamp	tent	sink	pond	tusk
	bank	felt	milk	frost	bump
	hand	vest	wind	cold	dust

Grammar sheet 23: The children read the outlined final blends and write inside them. Then they read the unfinished words and try adding the final blends to each of them. They try each final blend in turn until they find one which completes the word, e.g. 'be' and 'mp' makes 'bemp', which is not a real word, whereas 'be' and 'lt' makes 'belt', which is. Once they have found a blend to complete a word, the children write it in and draw a picture for the word. As long as the children have made real words, their answers are right, so 'sta' could become either 'stamp' or 'stand'.

Extension activity: Write the unfinished words and final blends out on cards. Give the cards out to the children. They see how many other words they can make. The Writing Master on page 172 may be photocopied onto the back of the grammar sheets for the children to write on. This exercise could be repeated with different unfinished words and final blends.

Rounding off: Go over the sheet with the children, seeing which words they made.

Final Blends

Try the different final blends until you find one that makes a word.
Write the blends in and draw pictures for the words you have made.

mp	lt	nt
st	nd	sp

sta_____

po_____

be_____

a_____

ne_____

ha _____

la_____

cri_____

te _____

Spelling 24 – ‹ew›

Prepare...
Flash cards:
• basic sounds
• new spellings
• tricky words
Spelling sheet 24
Spelling list 24
Jewel shape

Revision: Revise some basic sounds and the other spellings covered so far. Revise tricky words '**why**', '**where**', '**who**', '**which**', '**any**', '**many**', '**more**', '**before**', '**other**' and '**were**'.

Main point: Remind the children that the main ways of writing the /ue/ sound are ‹ue›, ‹u_e› and ‹ew›. However, ‹ew› is a difficult spelling because it often makes an /oo/ sound, as in 'grew'. Teach the ‹ew› spelling of the /ue/ and /oo/ sounds. With the children, make a list of words which use it. Then ask them to make up sentences, using some of the words. The words could also be written onto a big jewel shape.

Activity sheet: The children write inside the outlined ew. Then in each jewel they write an ‹ew› word and draw a picture for that word. Afterwards they colour the sheet.

Dictation: Read the words and sentences for the children to write down. The Dictation Master on page 171 may be photocopied onto the back of the spelling sheets for the children to write on.

Spelling list: Read the spelling words with the children. As a class, call out the sounds in the regular words, and say the letter names for the tricky words '**because**' and '**want**'. For 'because', tell the children to use the mnemonic '**b**ig **e**lephants **c**atch **a**nts **u**nder **s**mall **e**lephants'. For 'want' the children should use the 'Say as it Sounds' method, pronouncing it to rhyme with 'ant'. The longer word 'newspaper' has three syllables and can be remembered as 'news', 'pa' and 'per', for spelling.

Dictation

1. few
2. new
3. pew
4. grew
5. chew
6. drew

1. A few more can go.
2. There is my new bike.
3. He drew a newt.

Spelling List 24

1. bud
2. sun
3. he**l**d
4. few
5. flew
6. grew
7. chew
8. **because**
9. **want**
10. newspaper

Write an ‹**ew**› word and draw a picture in each jewel.

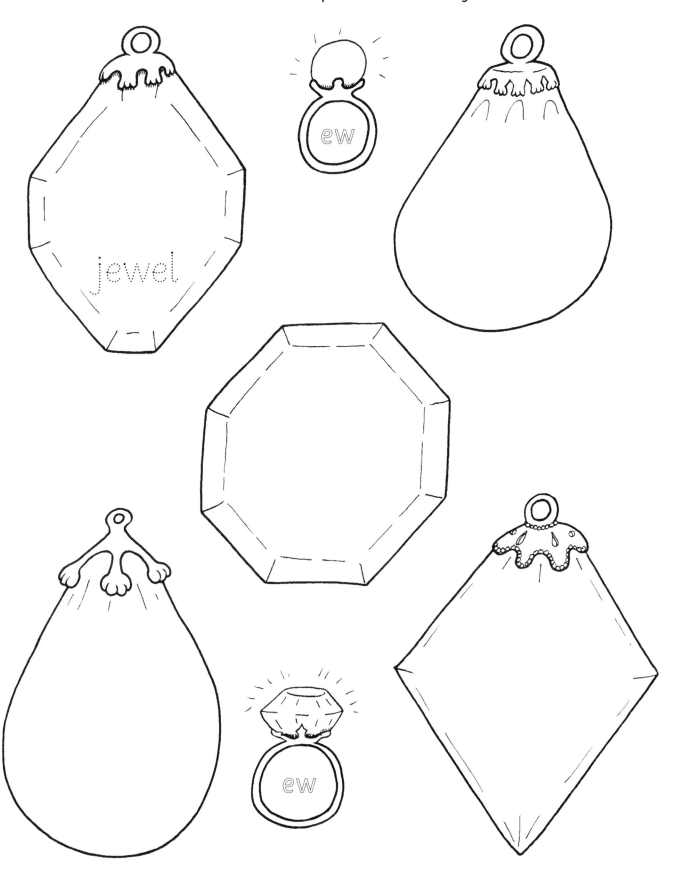

jewel

ew

ew

Action: Move head forward as if it is the cuckoo, saying *oo*. (This comes from the action for *u oo*.)

Action: Point to people around you and say *you, you*.

Spelling sheet 24

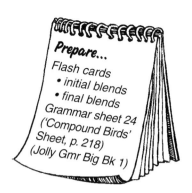

Prepare...
Flash cards
• initial blends
• final blends
Grammar sheet 24
('Compound Birds'
Sheet, p. 218)
(Jolly Gmr Big Bk 1)

Grammar 24 – Compound Words

Aim: Develop the children's ability to recognise compound words.

Introduction: Revise initial and final blends. Hold up flash cards of the blends for the children to read. Then call out blends for the children to name the letters in them.

Main point: Compound words are words made of two (or more) shorter words joined together. Draw some 'picture word sums' on the board for the children to work out the compound words. Alternatively look at the compound birds page in the *Jolly Grammar Big Book 1*. You could also use the Red Level *Jolly Readers* 'Star and Fish'.

Example: picture of egg   +   picture of cup   =   'eggcup'

Other words which could be used:

blue + bell	star + fish	foot + ball
tooth + brush	black + bird	cow + boy/girl
sun + flower	arm + chair	ear + ring
rain + coat	sea + shell	butter + fly

Grammar sheet 24: The children read the words in the birds' wings and tails. Then they try adding the 'tail words' to the 'wing words' to make compound words. They try each 'tail word' in turn until they find one that makes sense, e.g. 'post' and 'ball' makes 'postball' which is not a real word, whereas 'post' and 'man' makes 'postman'.

Extension activity: Give the children some more words, on the board or on cards, and see how many compound words they can make using them. The 'Compound Birds' sheet on page 218 may be photocopied and cut up to make sets of compound word puzzles.

Examples:		
rain + bow	shoe + lace	lunch + time
lunch + box	home + work	home + time
shoe + box	letter + box	fire + work

Rounding off: Go over the sheet with the children, seeing which compound words they made.

Compound Words

The compound birds have muddled up their tails.
Can you sort them out?

post

foot

sun

green

tooth

tea

ball

set

brush

pot

man

house

Spelling 25 – ‹ou›

Prepare...
Flash cards:
• basic sounds
• new spellings
• tricky words
Spelling sheet 25
Spelling list 25
House shape

Revision: Revise some basic sounds and the other spellings covered so far. Revise tricky words 'who', 'which', 'any', 'many', 'more', 'before', 'other', 'were', 'because' and 'want'.

Main point: Remind the children that the main ways of writing the /ou/ sound are ‹ou› and ‹ow›. Revise the ‹ou› spelling of the /ou/ sound. With the children, make a list of words which use it. Then ask them to make up sentences, using some of the words. The words could also be written onto a big house shape.

Spelling sheet 25: The children write inside the outlined ou. Then in each house they write an ‹ou› word and draw a picture for that word. Afterwards they colour the sheet.

Dictation: Read the words and sentences for the children to write down. The Dictation Master on page 171 may be photocopied onto the back of the spelling sheets for the children to write on.

Spelling list: Read the spelling words with the children. As a class, call out the sounds in the regular words, and say the letter names for the tricky words 'saw' and 'put'. The longer word 'outside' is a compound word. It has two syllables and can be remembered as 'out' and 'side' for spelling.

Dictation	
1. our	4. flour
2. loud	5. found
3. south	6. round

1. The hoop is round.
2. Mum needs some flour to make a cake.
3. He counted to fifty.

Spelling List 25
1. bat
2. pet
3. self
4. out
5. our
6. round
7. mouth
8. **saw**
9. **put**
10. outside

Write an ‹**ou**› word and draw a picture in each house.

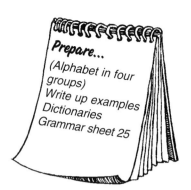

Prepare...
(Alphabet in four groups)
Write up examples
Dictionaries
Grammar sheet 25

Grammar 25 – Alphabetical order

Aim: Develop the children's knowledge of the alphabet, and their ability to put words into alphabetical order.

Introduction: The children sit in a circle, and one child says the first letter of the alphabet. Go round the circle with each child saying the next letter. Then the children practise saying the alphabet in the four groups. They hold up one finger as they say the first group, pause, then hold up two fingers as they say the second, etc.

Main point: Write some words on the board. For simplicity, make sure each word begins with a different letter. With the children's help, put the words into alphabetical order. Then write a word on the board that the children will recognise even though it is deliberately mis-spelt, e.g. 'mumy'. Ask if the word is spelt correctly. Tell the children that if they are not sure whether a spelling is correct, they can check it with a dictionary. Look up the word in the dictionary and read out the letters, asking the children to check the spelling on the board. Explain that if they do not know how a word is spelt but can sound out the first few letters, then they will probably be able to find it in a dictionary.

Grammar sheet 25: The children put each group of words into alphabetical order. Then they can write inside the outlined alphabet, and look at the pictures at the bottom of the sheet. They try writing a word for each, and then check in a dictionary to see if they have spelt them correctly. Although the children may not know how to spell the word 'television', they will probably be able to sound out the first few letters. If these words are not in the children's dictionaries then the pictures could be replaced, or the exercise could be treated as a whole-class activity, using a dictionary which does contain the words.

Extension activity: Draw pictures on the board. The chidren write words for the pictures and check their spellings in a dictionary.

Rounding off: Go over the sheet with the children. Call out letters and see if the children can find the right section for them in the dictionary.

Alphabetical Order

Put these words into alphabetical order.

1. car   tractor   lorry

   _____   _____   _____

2. hamster   cat   rabbit

   _____   _____   _____

3. lemon   apple   banana

   _____   _____   _____

4. Sam   Alex   Ravi   Gilbert

   _____   _____   _____   _____

5. Emily   Pat   Davinda   Sue   Jill

   _____   _____   _____   _____   _____

Look up the words for these nouns in your dictionary.
Copy the words out carefully.

_____   _____

ABCDEFGHIJKLMNOPQRSTUVWXYZ

Spelling 26 – ‹ow›

Prepare...
Flash cards:
• basic sounds
• new spellings
• tricky words
Spelling sheet 26
Spelling list 26
Owl shape

Revision: Revise some basic sounds and the other spellings covered so far. Revise tricky words 'any', 'many', 'more', 'before', 'other', 'were', 'because', 'want', 'saw' and 'put'.

Main point: Remind the children that the main ways of writing the /ou/ sound are ‹ou› and ‹ow›. Revise the ‹**ow**› spelling of the /ou/ sound. With the children, make a list of words which use it. Then ask them to make up sentences, using some of the words. The words could also be written onto a big owl shape.

Spelling sheet 26: The children write inside the outlined ow. Then in each owl they write an ‹ow› word and draw a picture to go with it. Afterwards they colour the sheet.

Dictation: Read the words and sentences for the children to write down. The Dictation Master on page 171 may be photocopied onto the back of the spelling sheets for the children to write on.

Spelling list: Read the spelling words with the children. As a class, call out the sounds in the regular words, and say the letter names for the tricky words '**could**' and '**should**'. Both spellings can be learnt with the mnemonic '**o u** lucky **d**uck'. The longer word 'flowerpot' is a compound word. It has three syllables and can be remembered as 'flow', 'er' and 'pot', for spelling.

Dictation

1. cow
2. now
3. clown
4. howl
5. crowd
6. powder

1. Come down here.
2. They went to town on the bus.
3. She had a quick shower.

Spelling List 26

1. big
2. fox
3. mi**lk**
4. how
5. owl
6. brown
7. town
8. **could**
9. **should**
10. flowerpot

Write an ‹**ow**› word and draw a picture in each owl.

ow

ow

owl

Action: Pretend your finger is a needle and prick your thumb saying *ou, ou, ou.*

Prepare...
Write up examples
Grammar sheet 26
Red pencils
(Jolly Grammar
Big Book 1)

Grammar 26 – Verbs

Aim: Develop the children's understanding of verbs, and their ability to identify verbs in sentences.

Introduction: Revise the parts of speech covered so far: proper and common nouns, pronouns, verbs and adjectives. You could use the pages in the *Jolly Grammar Big Book 1* to help you do this. Call out words for the children to do the appropriate actions. Remember that some words can function as both nouns and verbs, so the children can do both actions.

Main point: Revise verbs. Look at the picture on Grammar sheet 26. Ask the children to give examples of verbs. Remind them that if we can put the word 'to' before a word, then it is probably a verb. Write some sentences on the board. Go through the sentences, finding the verbs with the children.

Examples: The girls jump in the water.
               The dog chews his bone.

Underline the verbs in red.

Grammar sheet 26: The children look at the picture and write six verbs for the actions they can see. Then they read the sentences underneath and underline the verbs in red. Tell them that there can be more than one verb in a sentence.

Extension activity: The children write some sentences about the picture and underline the verbs. The Writing Master on page 172 may be photocopied onto the back of the grammar sheets for the children to write on. The children could also look up their six verbs in the dictionary.

Rounding off: Go over the sheet, with the children identifying the verbs.

Verbs

Write 6 verbs for actions you can see in the picture.

to _____   to _____

to _____   to _____

to _____   to _____

Underline the verbs in these sentences in red.
There can be more than one verb in a sentence.

1. Jenny smiled at her friend.

2. Alex sails a boat.

3. Hannah swims and dives in the sea.

4. The boys make a big sand castle and then play ball.

Spelling 27 – ‹oi›

Prepare...
Flash cards:
• basic sounds
• new spellings
• tricky words
Spelling sheet 27
Spelling list 27
Oil-can shape

Revision: Revise some basic sounds and the other spellings covered so far. Revise tricky words '**more**', '**before**', '**other**', '**were**', '**because**', '**want**', '**saw**', '**put**', '**could**' and '**should**'.

Main point: Remind the children that the main ways of writing the /oi/ sound are ‹oi› and ‹oy›. Revise the ‹**oi**› spelling of the /oi/ sound. With the children, make a list of words which use it. Then ask them to make up sentences, using some of the words. The words could also be written onto a big oil-can shape.

Spelling sheet 27: The children write inside the outlined oi. Then in each oil can they write an ‹oi› word, and draw a picture for that word. Afterwards they colour the sheet.

Dictation: Read the words and sentences for the children to write down. The Dictation Master on page 171 may be photocopied onto the back of the spelling sheets for the children to write on.

Spelling list: Read the spelling words with the children. As a class, call out the sounds in the regular words, and say the letter names for the tricky words '**would**' and '**right**'. 'Would' can be learnt with the mnemonic '**o u** lucky **d**uck'. 'Right' is not really a tricky word, but the children need to remember that the /ie/ sound is made with the ‹igh› spelling. The longer word 'boiling' has two syllables and can be remembered as 'boil' and 'ing' for spelling.

Dictation

1. boil
2. join
3. soil
4. joint
5. foil
6. spoil

1. It was a noisy car.
2. They are pointing at me.
3. He needed the toilet.

Spelling List 27

1. bug
2. had
3. **film**
4. oil
5. coin
6. noisy
7. toilet
8. **would**
9. **right**
10. boiling

Write an ‹oi› word and draw a picture in each oil can.

oi

oil

oi

Prepare...
Action picture
Grammar sheet 27
Orange pencils
(Jolly Grammar
Big Book 1)

Grammar 27 – Adverbs

Aim: Develop the children's understanding of adverbs. Adverbs are words which describe verbs.

Introduction: Revise verbs. Look at a picture showing lots of things happening. Ask the children for verbs for some of them. Make up some sentences using the verbs and write them on the board. Underline the verbs in red.

Examples: They swim.
              She sings.

Main point: Explain that just as adjectives describe nouns, there are also words which describe verbs. These words are called **adverbs**. There is a page in the *Jolly Grammar Big Book 1* that will help you introduce adverbs.

Action: The action for an adverb is to bang one fist on top of the other.

Colour: The colour for adverbs is orange.

With the children, think of adverbs to describe the verbs in the sentences on the board, e.g. 'They swim quickly', 'She sings loudly'. Underline the adverbs in orange.

Grammar sheet 27: The children read the adverbs at the top of the sheet and the unfinished sentences under the pictures. Then they decide which adverb could be used to complete each sentence. They can either copy the adverbs, or cut them out and stick them into the spaces provided.

Extension activity: Write some verbs on the board and ask the children to think of an adverb to describe each one.

Examples: speak   swim   sing   build   clean   paint   drive   play

Rounding off: Go over the sheet with the children. Their answers are right so long as the adverbs chosen make sense in the sentences.

Adverbs  *Orange*

.Choose an adverb to go with each picture.

secretly	happily	quickly
hungrily	loudly	slowly

Inky eats

Snake slithers

Bee buzzes

The ants whisper

Snail goes

The band played

Action: Bang one fist on top of the other.

Colour: Orange

Spelling 28 – ‹oy›

Prepare...
Flash cards:
• basic sounds
• new spellings
• tricky words
Spelling sheet 28
Spelling list 28
Toy shape

Revision: Revise some basic sounds and the other Spellings covered so far.   Revise tricky words 'other', 'were', 'because', 'want', 'saw', 'put', 'could', 'should', 'would' and 'right'.

Main point: Remind the children that the main ways of writing the /oi/ sound are ‹oi› and ‹oy›. Revise the ‹oy› spelling of the /oi/ sound. Tell the children that the ‹oy› spelling is usually used at the end of words. The ‹y› takes the place of (shy) ‹i›. The letter ‹i› does not like to be at the end of words. With the children, make a list of words which use ‹oy›. Then ask them to make up sentences, using some of the words. The words could also be written onto a bit toy shape.

Examples: boy   enjoy   annoy
                 toy   destroy   royal
                 joy   employ   loyal

Spelling sheet 28:   The children write inside the outlined ‹oy›. Then in each toy they write an ‹oy› word and draw a picture for that word. Afterwards they colour the sheet.

Dictation: Read the words and sentences for the children to write down. The Dictation Master on page 171 may be photocopied onto the back of the spelling sheets for the children to write on.

Spelling list: Read the spelling words with the children. As a class, call out the sounds in the regular words, and say the letter names for the tricky words 'two' and 'four'. The longer word 'destroy' has two syllables and can be remembered as 'des' and 'troy' for spelling.

Dictation

1. boy   4. enjoy
2. toy   5. royal
3. joy   6. annoy

1. They enjoyed the trip.
2. The fly was annoying the boy.
3. His toy car had a crash.

Spelling List 28

1. jet
2. dig
3. he**lp**
4. boy
5. toy
6. enjoy
7. annoy
8. **two**
9. **four**
10. destroy

Write an ‹**oy**› word and draw a picture in each toy.

toy

oy

Prepare...
Grammar sheet 28
Orange pencils
(Jolly Grammar
Big Book 1)

Grammar 28 – Adverbs

Aim: Develop the children's understanding of adverbs.

Introduction: Revise verbs. Talk about Inky, Snake and Bee, (or some of the children). With the children, decide where they might go for an outing, e.g. to the park or to the seaside. Think of things they might do, e.g. climb up the slide or build a sand castle. Make a list of these activities on the board.

Main point: Revise adverbs. With the children, think of some adverbs to describe the verbs listed on the board.

Grammar sheet 28: The children read the adverbs, at the top of the sheet, and the story in the beehive. Then they decide which adverb could be used to fill each gap.

Extension activity: The children write, or draw a picture, about what they think Inky, Snake and Bee might do on their day out. The Writing Master on page 172 may be photocopied onto the back of the grammar sheets for the children to write on.

Rounding off: Go over the sheet with the children. Their answers are right as long as the adverbs chosen make sense in the sentences. Ask the children where they think Inky, Snake and Bee went.

Adverds

Orange

Read these adverbs, then read the story in the beehive.
Write an adverb in each space.

loudly	soon	suddenly
quickly	happily	slowly

Bee's Busy Day

Bee woke up _____,
and crawled _____ down
the hive to have breakfast.
She buzzed _____ as she
flew to the farm. She _____
collected as much pollen as she
could, and flew _____ back to
the hive. She smiled _____ to
herself. Bee, and her friends Inky
and Snake, had planned a day out.

Spelling 29 – ‹or›

Prepare...
Flash cards:
• basic sounds
• new spellings
• tricky words
Spelling sheet 29
Spelling list 29
Horse shape

Revision: Revise some basic sounds and the other spellings covered so far. Revise tricky words 'because', 'want', 'saw', 'put', 'could', 'should', 'would', 'right', 'two' and 'four'.

Main point: Remind the children that the main ways of writing the /or/ sound are ‹or›, ‹al›, ‹au› and ‹aw›. Revise the ‹or› spelling of the /or/ sound. With the children, make a list of words which use it. Then ask them to make up sentences, using some of the words. The words could also be written onto a big horse shape.

Spelling sheet 29: The children write inside the outlined or. Then in each horse they write an ‹or› word and draw a picture for that word. Afterwards they colour the sheet.

Dictation: Read the words and sentences for the children to write down. The Dictation Master on page 171 may be photocopied onto the back of the spelling sheets for the children to write on.

Spelling list: Read the spelling words with the children. As a class, call out the sounds in the regular words, and say the letter names for the tricky words **'goes'** and **'does'**. The longer word 'morning' has two syllables and can be remembered as 'mor' and 'ning' for spelling.

Dictation

1. corn
2. sort
3. worn
4. torch
5. for
6. sport

1. The farmer cut the corn.
2. I will sort those out in the morning.
3. There is going to be a storm.

Spelling List 29

1. got
2. bun
3. belt
4. fork
5. storm
6. horse
7. forty
8. **goes**
9. **does**
10. morning

Write an ‹**or**› word and draw a picture in each horse.

 Action: Put hands on head as if donkey's ears pointing down, and say *or*. (This comes from the *ee or* action.)

Grammar 29 – ‹es› Plurals

Aim: Develop the children's understanding of singular and plural, and their knowledge that, if a word ends in ‹sh›, ‹ch›, ‹s› or ‹x›, the plural is made by adding ‹es›.

Introduction: Revise singular and plural. Write some sentences on the board.

Examples: The dog barked loudly.
             The cat walked slowly.

With the children, identify the parts of speech and underline them in the appropriate colours. Then ask the children to make the nouns plural.

Main point: Tell the children that if a word ends in ‹sh›, ‹ch›, ‹s› or ‹x›, then the plural is made by adding ‹**es**›.

Examples:	wish	church	dress	box
	dish	bunch	kiss	fox
	crash	catch	pass	six
	brush	ditch	class	fix

Grammar sheet 29: The children write inside the outlined letters in the left-hand boxes. Then they choose a noun for each spelling and write it in the central box. They write the plural of the noun in the right-hand box and draw a picture for each word. Remind the children that the picture for each plural must show more than one item. They can cut their sheets as indicated and put the four sections in a pile. Each pile can be stapled on the dotted line on the left-hand side, to make a little book with the ‹sh› on top. Fold the four pages as indicated, so they can be unfolded to reveal 'brush' and 'brushes', etc.

Extension activity: Write some sentences on the board which use nouns in the singular. Ask the children to write the sentences in the plural. Either use only ‹es› plurals, or mix them up with regular ‹s› plurals. Alternatively the children could think of as many words as they can that end with ‹sh›, ‹ch›, ‹s› or ‹x›.

Rounding off: Call out some nouns, some of which need ‹es› and some of which need ‹s› to make the plural. The children listen carefully to each word and say which letter(s) should be added.

‹es› plurals

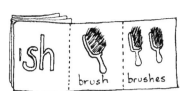

sh

Staple ••••••••••

brush   brushes

ch

Staple ••••••••••

s

Staple ••••••••••

x

Staple ••••••••••

Spelling 30 – ‹al›

Prepare...
Flash cards:
• basic sounds
• new spellings
• tricky words
Spelling sheet 30
Spelling list 30
Talk-bubble shape

Revision: Revise some basic sounds and the other spellings covered so far. Revise tricky words '**saw**', '**put**', '**could**', '**should**', '**would**', '**right**', '**two**', '**four**', '**goes**' and '**does**'.

Main point: Remind the children that the main ways of writing the /or/ sound are ‹or›, ‹al›, ‹au› and ‹aw›. Revise the ‹al› spelling of the /or/ sound. With the children, make a list of words which use it. Then ask them to make up sentences, using some of the words. The words could also be written onto a talk-bubble shape.

Spelling sheet 30: The children write inside the outlined al. Then in each talk bubble they write an ‹al› word and draw a picture to go with it. Afterwards they colour the sheet.

Dictation: Read the words and sentences for the children to write down. The Dictation Master on page 171 may be photocopied onto the back of the spelling sheets for the children to write on.

Spelling list: Read the spelling words with the children. As a class, call out the sounds in the regular words, and say the letter names for the tricky words '**made**' and '**their**'. 'Made' is not really a tricky word, but the children need to remember that the /ai/ sound is made with the ‹a_e› spelling. For 'their', tell the children that this spelling is used for belonging, e.g. 'their clothes', 'their toys'. The longer word 'beanstalk' is a compound word. It has two syllables and can be remembered as 'bean' and 'stalk' for spelling.

Dictation

1. also
2. talk
3. always
4. falling
5. ball
6. wall

1. They took a short walk.
2. He always hit the ball.
3. I grew a tall beanstalk.

Spelling List 30

1. bad
2. vet
3. **fact**
4. all
5. talk
6. walk
7. small
8. **made**
9. **their**
10. beanstalk

Write an ‹**al**› word and draw a picture in each talk bubble.

 Action: Put hands on head as if donkey's ears pointing down, and say *or*. (This comes from the *ee or* action.)

Prepare...
Write up examples
Grammar sheet 30
(Antonym cards)

Grammar 30 – Antonyms

Aim: Develop the children's understanding of antonyms, which is another word for opposites.

Introduction: Give a few examples of antonyms, or opposites, e.g. 'big / small', 'dark / light', 'up / down'. Call out some words and ask for their antonyms. Then see if they can suggest any antonym pairs themselves.

Main point: Write some sentences on the board and read them with the children.

Example: 'A tall man drove backwards out of his garage and on to a rough road. At the roundabout he turned right. It was a dark, wet night. He made a quick turn at a small bend in the road and hit a low wall. The car went over the wall and stopped.'

With the children, identify those words which have antonyms. Try putting the antonyms into the sentences and see if the story still makes sense.

Grammar sheet 30: The children read each word, and write its antonym on the line in the opposite half of the box. They draw a picture for each antonym.

Extension activity: Write some jumbled antonyms on the board, for the children to identify the pairs, and write them down. Alternatively the antonyms could be written on cards for the children to sort into pairs.

Examples: backwards / forwards   right / wrong   good / bad
rough / smooth   sharp / blunt   fat / thin
flat / round   easy / hard   wet / dry
slow / quick   right / left   high / low
dark / light   over / under   small / large
long / short   liquid / solid   little / big

Rounding off: Call out some phrases or sentences which use words with antonyms. Ask the children to replace these words with their antonyms, e.g. 'a big dog' / 'a small dog'; 'He walked slowly' / 'He walked quickly'; 'an easy sum' / 'a hard sum'.

Opposites   Antonyms

Write each opposite and draw a picture.

white
_____

day
_____

hot
_____

quiet
_____

up
_____

hard
_____

asleep
_____

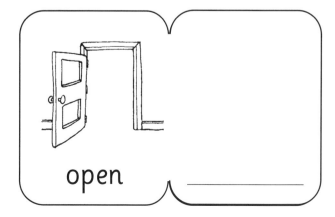
open
_____

Spelling 31 – ‹nk›

Prepare...
Flash cards:
• basic sounds
• new spellings
• tricky words
Spelling sheet 31
Spelling list 31
Drink shape

Revision: Revise some basic sounds and the other spellings covered so far. Revise tricky words '**could**', '**should**', '**would**', '**right**', '**two**', '**four**', '**goes**', '**does**', '**made**' and '**their**'.

Main point: Teach the ‹nk› spelling of the combined sounds /ng/ and /k/. When together these sounds are nearly always written as ‹nk›, so it is an important spelling pattern to learn. With the children, make a list of words which use ‹nk›. Then ask them to make up sentences, using some of the words. The words could also be written onto a big drink shape.

Spelling sheet 31: The children write inside the outlined nk. Then in each drink they write an ‹nk› word, and draw a picture for that word. Afterwards they colour the sheet.

Dictation: Read the words and sentences for the children to write down. The Dictation Master on page 171 may be photocopied onto the back of the spelling sheets for the children to write on.

Spelling list: Read the spelling words with the children. As a class, call out the sounds in the regular words, and say the letter names for the tricky words '**once**' and '**upon**'. The longer word 'thinking' has two syllables and can be remembered as 'think' and 'ing' for spelling.

Dictation

1. ink
2. rink
3. blink
4. trunk
5. drank
6. shrink

1. The pink pig blinked.
2. What would you like to drink?
3. I sleep in the top bunk.

Spelling List 31

1. fin
2. sob
3. **left**
4. sink
5. pink
6. drink
7. thank
8. **once**
9. **upon**
10. thinking

Write an ‹**nk**› word and draw a picture in each drink.

drink

nk

nk

Grammar 31 – Alphabetical order

Prepare...
(Alphabet in four groups)
Write up examples
Dictionaries
Grammar sheet 31
(Coloured pencils)

Aim: Develop the children's knowledge of the alphabet, and their ability to use word books and dictionaries.

Introduction: The children sit in a circle and say the letters of the alphabet in turn. Then they practise saying the alphabet in the four groups. They hold up one finger as they say the first group, pause, then hold up two fingers as they say the second, etc. Call out letters. Ask the children which group each letter belongs to, e.g. 's' is in group 3. Knowing where a letter falls in the alphabet will help the children work out where to look for it in the dictionary. Call out a letter and ask the children to say which letter comes before it and which after it. Repeat with other letters.

Main point: Tell the children that they can use a dictionary to help them if they are not sure how a word is spelt. Explain that they will need to sound out the first few letters of the word, find the appropriate section of the dictionary, and then look for the word. If they have already written a word but decide that it looks wrong, they can check the spelling by looking up the word in the dictionary.

Write a few words on the board, mis-spelling some of them. (Make sure all the words are included in the dictionaries used.)

Examples: leter   animal   biskit

Ask the children whether they think the words are spelt correctly. Then look the words up in a dictionary and correct them with the children.

Grammar sheet 31: There are two spellings underneath each picture. The children read them, then look up the word in the dictionary and tick the correct spelling. The three words in the middle have been mis-spelt. The children look up these words and correct the spellings. They can use coloured pencils to make their corrections clear. Then the children look up the last two words on the sheet, and copy out the meanings given in their dictionaries. Make sure all the words are included in the dictionaries used. If a word is not included, replace it with one that is.

Extension activity: Write some more words on the board and ask the children to find out what they mean. The words could be related to a topic the children are studying.

Rounding off: Go over the sheet with the children, checking the spellings and meanings of the words.

Using a Dictionary

We can use a dictionary to check how to spell words.
Look up each word in your dictionary to choose the right spelling.

toofbrush
toothbrush

rabbit
rabit

starr
star

octopus
octapus

flouer
flower

buterfie
butterfly

These words are spelt wrongly. Look them up and copy them correctly.

boock   **carpit**   **triangel**

_____   _____   _____

You can also use a dictionary to find the meaning of a word.
Look up these words and write down what they mean.

atlas _____

_____

yacht _____

_____

Spelling 32 – ‹er›

Prepare...
Flash cards:
• basic sounds
• new spellings
• tricky words
Spelling sheet 32
Spelling list 32
Gingerbread shape

Revision: Revise some basic sounds and the other spellings covered so far. Revise tricky words '**would**', '**right**', '**two**', '**four**', '**goes**', '**does**', '**made**', '**their**', '**once**' and '**upon**'.

Main point: Remind the children that the main ways of writing the /er/ sound are ‹er›, ‹ir› and ‹ur›. Revise the ‹er› spelling of the /er/ sound. The ‹er› spelling often comes at the end of words, where it makes a slightly shorter sound. With the children, make a list of words which use it. Then ask them to make up sentences, using some of the words. The words could also be written onto a big gingerbread shape.

Spelling sheet 32: The children write inside the outlined er. Then in each gingerbread person they write an ‹er› word, and draw a picture for that word. Afterwards they colour the sheet.

Dictation: Read the words and sentences for the children to write down. The Dictation Master on page 171 may be photocopied onto the back of the spelling sheets for the children to write on.

Spelling list: Read the spelling words with the children. As a class, call out the sounds in the regular words, and say the letter names for the tricky words '**always**' and '**also**'. It may help to tell the children that when 'all' is part of a compound word, it loses the second ‹l›. The longer word 'woodpecker' is also a compound word. It has three syllables and can be remembered as 'wood', 'peck' and 'er', for spelling.

Dictation

1. herb
2. fern
3. term
4. never
5. winter
6. silver

1. I grew some herbs.
2. Her ring is made of silver.
3. There are fish in the river.

Spelling List 32

1. mud
2. jam
3. se**nt**
4. term
5. summer
6. river
7. number
8. **always**
9. **also**
10. woodpecker

Write an ‹**er**› word and draw a picture in each gingerbread person.

term

er

er

 Action: Roll hands over each other like a mixer and say *erererer*.

Grammar 32 – Speech Marks

Prepare...
Comic with speech bubbles
Book with speech marks
Grammar sheet 32 (Write up examples)
Jolly Gmr Big Book 1

Aim: Develop the children's understanding of speech marks.

Introduction: Find a comic or book that uses speech bubbles. Ask the children what the speech bubbles are for. Read some of the speech in the bubbles. Draw a speech bubble on the board. Draw an animal or write its name. Ask the children what noise the animal makes. Write this in the speech bubble. Ask the children to think of some more animals and the sounds they make. Write some of these sounds in the speech bubble on the board.

Main Point: Now show the children a page of a book which has speech marks. Point out the speech marks and see if the children can say why they are there. Point out that the first word after the speech marks usually has a capital letter. Explain that the speech marks are used before and after anything that is actually spoken. The words that come out of our mouths are called 'speech' and it is only these words that go between the speech marks. It may help the children write the speech marks correctly, if they think of them as a '66' before the speech and a '99' after it. Read aloud from the book, with the children looking out for speech marks and reading the spoken words themselves. There is a page in the *Jolly Grammar Big Book 1* that will help you introduce speech marks.

Grammar sheet 32: The children write in the outlined speech marks. Then they think what noise each animal makes, e.g. 'Hiss' for the snake. They write the noise, first in the speech bubble and then in the box underneath. Remind them to start each one with a capital letter. In the first two examples, the speech marks are provided in outline. In the others, the children should write the speech marks themselves, in the circles provided.

Extension activity: Write some sentences on the board. The children copy the sentences and put in the speech marks.

Examples: Woof, woof said the dog.
              My cat is called Tolly said Bill.
              The girl said I like going to the beach.

Rounding off: Go over the sheet, with the children suggesting the sounds the animals might make. If there are sentences on the board, go over them, with the children adding the speech marks.

"Speech Marks"

said the snake.

said the cow.

said the bird.

said the bee.

said the duck.

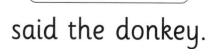
said the donkey.

Spelling 33 – ‹ir›

Prepare...
Flash cards:
• basic sounds
• new spellings
• tricky words
Spelling sheet 33
Spelling list 33
Bird shape

Revision: Revise some basic sounds and the other spellings covered so far. Revise tricky words 'two', 'four', 'goes', 'does', 'made', 'their', 'once' ,'upon', 'always' and 'also'.

Main point: Remind the children that the main ways of writing the /er/ sound are ‹er›, ‹ir› and ‹ur›. Revise the ‹ir› spelling of the /er/ sound. With the children, make a list of words which use it. Then ask them to make up sentences, using some of the words. The words could also be written onto a big bird shape. Tell the children that an /er/ sound in a number word will probably be spelt ‹ir›, e.g. 'first', 'third', 'thirteen' and 'thirty'.

Spelling sheet 33: The children write inside the outlined ir. Then in each bird they write an ‹ir› word, and draw a picture for that word. Afterwards they colour the sheet.

Dictation: Read the words and sentences for the children to write down. The Dictation Master on page 171 may be photocopied onto the back of the spelling sheets for the children to write on.

Spelling list: Read the spelling words with the children. As a class, call out the sounds in the regular words, and say the letter names for the tricky words 'of' and 'eight'. Remind the children to write 'of' with an ‹f›, although it has a /v/ sound at the end. The longer word 'birthday' is a compound word. It has two syllables and can be remembered as 'birth' and 'day' for spelling.

Dictation

1. dirt
2. stir
3. sir
4. third
5. thirty
6. bird

1. The girl is thirsty.
2. When is your birthday?
3. I have a green skirt and red shirt.

Spelling List 33

1. yet
2. hid
3. we**pt**
4. skirt
5. girl
6. shirt
7. first
8. **of**
9. **eight**
10. birthday

Write an ‹**ir**› word and draw a picture in each bird.

 Action: Roll hands over each other like a mixer and say *erererer.*

Prepare...
Write up example
Grammar sheet 33
(Thesauruses)
Big word web

Grammar 33 – Word Web

Aim: Encourage the children to think about the words they choose to use in their writing.

Introduction: Explain that some words can have the same or similar meanings as each other, e.g. 'happy', 'jolly', 'cheerful' and 'merry'. Ask the children if they can think of any other words which mean 'happy'. Then ask if they can think of similar meanings for other words.

Examples: sad   hot   dirty   small   big   hurry   horrible

The children could also be shown a thesaurus. Explain that it is a special book which tells us about words with similar meanings.

Main Point: Tell the children that they can make their writing more interesting by thinking carefully about the words they use, and by avoiding using the same word over and over again. One word which is often overused is 'said'. Write a sentence on the board, reminding the children about speech marks.

Example: "Where are you going?" said Jim.

Encourage the children to think of the different ways Jim might say this, and the different words they could use.

Examples:	asked	replied	called	shouted	cried
	whispered	roared	murmured	explained	yelled
	screamed	answered	muttered	wondered	hissed

Grammar sheet 33: The children write a word that could be used instead of 'said', in each section of the word web. They could look in books to find more examples.

Extension activity: Let the children look at, and read some thesauruses.

Rounding off: See how many different words the children have thought of, or found. Make a class collection on a big 'word web'.

Word Web

How many words can you think of that you could use instead of 'said'?
Write the words in the spaces of the word web.

Spelling 34 – ‹ur›

Prepare...
Flash cards:
• basic sounds
• new spellings
• tricky words
Spelling sheet 34
Spelling list 34
Turkey shape

Revision: Revise some basic sounds and the other spellings covered so far. Revise tricky words **'goes'**, **'does'**, **'made'**, **'their'**, **'once'**, **'upon'**, **'always'**, **'also'**, **'of'** and **'eight'**.

Main point: Remind the children that the main ways of writing the /er/ sound are ‹er›, ‹ir› and ‹ur›. Revise the ‹**ur**› spelling of the /er/ sound. With the children, make a list of words which use it. Then ask them to make up sentences, using some of the words. The words could also be written onto a big turkey shape. Tell the children that two days of the week take the ‹ur› spelling: 'Saturday' and 'Thursday'.

Spelling sheet 34: The children write inside the outlined ur. Then in each turkey they write a ‹ur› word, and draw a picture to go with it. Afterwards they colour the sheet.

Dictation: Read the words and sentences for the children to write down. The Dictation Master on page 171 may be photocopied onto the back of the spelling sheets for the children to write on.

Spelling list: Read the spelling words with the children. As a class, call out the sounds in the regular words, and say the letter names for the tricky words **'love'** and **'cover'**. The longer word 'hamburger' is a compound word. It has three syllables and can be remembered as 'ham', 'bur' and 'ger', for spelling. Point out that the /er/ sound in the middle of the word is spelt ‹ur›, but the /er/ sound at the end is spelt ‹er›.

Dictation

1. fur
2. burn
3. hurt
4. burst
5. curly
6. turning

1. The nurse visited on Thursday.
2. We always have burnt toast.
3. It is your turn next.

Spelling List 34

1. not
2. sum
3. ne**x**t
4. turn
5. nurse
6. turkey
7. purple
8. **love**
9. **cover**
10. hamburger

Write a ‹**ur**› word and draw a picture in each turkey.

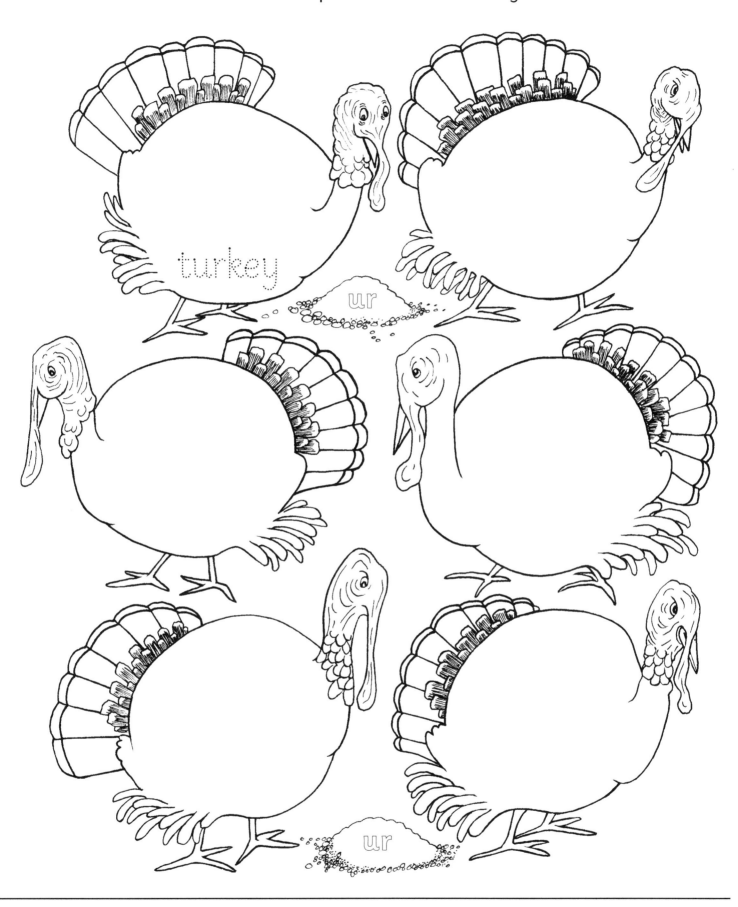

Action: Roll hands over each other like a mixer and say *erererer.*

Grammar 34 – Questions

Prepare...
Write up months
Write up question
Grammar sheet 34

Aim: Develop the children's understanding of questions, and of when to use question marks.

Introduction: Sit the children in a circle. Have the months of the year written out for the children to see. Read them with the children. Go round the circle, with each child in turn saying the next month. Then go round the circle asking each child 'When is your birthday?'

Main Point: Write the question 'When is your birthday?' on the board. Ask the children if they know what the mark at the end of the sentence is. Explain that it is a question mark and that it tells us that the sentence is a question. Demonstrate how to write a question mark. Write the ‹wh› question words on the board: 'what', 'why', 'when', 'where', 'who' and 'which'. Read the words with the children. Usually when we ask a question, we expect an answer, as questions can be used to get information. The children learnt when each others' birthdays were by asking the question 'When is your birthday?' Ask them to imagine meeting someone for the first time. What other questions could they ask, to find out more about that person?

Grammar sheet 34: With the children, go through the sheet, reading the question words. The children write inside the outlined question words and the ?, using coloured pencils if they prefer. Remind them to start the question marks at the top. Next they answer the three questions about themselves. Then they think of some questions they could ask someone they had just met for the first time, to find out more about that person.

Extension activity: The children think of as many questions as they can. Then they could take turns asking questions with a partner.

Rounding off: Go round the class, asking the children for their questions.

? Questions

Question words

what   why   when
where   who   which

Go over the question marks, using different colours.

? ? ? ? ? ? ? ? ? ?

Answer these questions.

1. What is your name? _____ _____

2. Where do you live? _____

3. When is your birthday? _____

? ? ? ? ? ? ? ? ? ?

If you met someone for the first time, what other questions could you ask them?

_____

_____

_____

Spelling 35 – ‹au›

Revision: Revise some basic sounds and the other spellings covered so far. Revise tricky words '**made**', '**their**', '**once**' ,'**upon**', '**always**', '**also**', '**of**', '**eight**', '**love**' and '**cover**'.

Main point: Remind the children that the main ways of writing the /or/ sound are ‹or›, ‹al›, ‹au› and ‹aw›. Revise the ‹au› spelling of the /or/ sound. With the children, make a list of words which use it. Then ask them to make up sentences, using some of the words. The words could also be written onto a big astronaut shape.

Examples: haul   haunt   fault   pause
             laundry   astronaut   Autumn   August

Spelling sheet 35: The children write inside the outlined au. Then in each astronaut they write an ‹au› word, and draw a picture for that word. Afterwards they colour the sheet.

Dictation: Read the words and sentences for the children to write down. The Dictation Master on page 171 may be photocopied onto the back of the spelling sheets for the children to write on.

Spelling list: Read the spelling words with the children. As a class, call out the sounds in the regular words, and say the letter names for the tricky words '**after**' and '**every**'. The longer word 'astronaut' has three syllables and can be remembered 'as', 'tron' and 'aut', for spelling.

Dictation

1. haul
2. fault
3. haunt
4. August
5. launch
6. vault

1. They always go there in August.
2. It was her fault.
3. Once I saw an astronaut.

Spelling List 35

1. map
2. fix
3. ju**mp**
4. fault
5. autumn
6. haunt
7. August
8. **after**
9. **every**
10. astronaut

Write an ‹**au**› word and draw a picture in each astronaut.

sauce

au

au

Action: Put hands on head as if donkey's ears pointing down, and say *or*. (This comes from the *ee or* action.)

Grammar 35 – Questions

Aim: Develop the children's understanding and use of questions.

Introduction: Ask the children some questions, e.g. 'What is your favourite colour?' 'Where did you go on holiday?' 'Who is your best friend?' 'When is your birthday?' 'Which drink do you like better – orange or blackcurrant?' Revise the ‹wh› question words, and write them on the board: 'what', 'why', 'when', 'where', 'who' and 'which'.

Write questions on the board with the question words missing.

Examples: '_____ do you live?' (Answer: 'where')
              '_____ is your party?' (Answer: 'when')
              '_____ likes chocolate?" (Answer: 'who')

Ask which question word would fit in each sentence. With the children, try inserting each of the questions words in turn, to see if they make sense.

Main Point: Show the children pictures of animals. Ask one child to choose an animal, but not to say which it is. The others ask questions to find out which animal it is. Remind the children that questions are usually asked to get information. The children will need to think carefully about which questions to ask, to find out as much as possible about the animal. They must not guess which it is, until five questions have been asked. This is a simplified version of the game '20 questions', and the rules can be adapted to suit the class. It can be played in spare moments, and can become more like '20 questions' as the children improve at asking questions.

Grammar sheet 35: Read through the sheet with the children. They choose a ‹wh› question word that makes sense to complete each of the questions. Then they read the questions and answers underneath to work out which animal has been chosen.

Extension activity: The children play the 'What am I?' game in pairs.

Rounding off: Go over the sheet with the children.

Questions

? Questions **?**

You ask questions to find things out.

what   where   when   why   who   which

Choose a question word to fit the sentences.

1. _____ won the quiz?

2. _____ time is it?

3. _____ book do you like best?

4. _____ are you going on holiday?

5. _____ did you do that?

6. _____ can we play tennis?

Read the questions and answers and see if you can guess the animal the girl is pretending to be.

1. Do you have fur?   Yes
2. How many legs do you have?   Four
3. What do you eat?   Carrots, oats and grass
4. Do you have long ears?   Yes

Which animal is it?   _____

Find a partner and play the game yourself.

Spelling 36 – ‹aw›

Prepare...
Flash cards:
• basic sounds
• new spellings
• tricky words
Spelling sheet 36
Spelling list 36
Saw shape

Revision: Revise some basic sounds and the other spellings. Revise tricky words **'once'**, **'upon'**, **'always'**, **'also'**, **'of'**, **'eight'**, **'love'**, **'cover'**, **'after'** and **'every'**.

Main point: Remind the children that the main ways of writing the /or/ sound are ‹or›, ‹al›, ‹au› and ‹aw›. Revise the **‹aw›** spelling of the /or/ sound. With the children, make a list of words which use it. Then ask them to make up sentences, using some of the words. The words could also be written onto a big saw shape.

Examples:

saw	law	paw	jaw	raw
claw	flaw	straw	draw	hawk
dawn	prawn	yawn	crawl	awful

Spelling sheet 36: The children write inside the outlined ⍺w. Then in each saw they write an ‹aw› word and draw a picture to go with it. Afterwards they colour the sheet.

Dictation: Read the words and sentences for the children to write down. The Dictation Master on page 171 may be photocopied onto the back of the spelling sheets for the children to write on.

Spelling list: Read the spelling words with the children. As a class, call out the sounds in the regular words, and say the letter names for the tricky words **'mother'** and **'father'**. The longer word 'strawberry' is a compound word. It has three syllables and can be remembered as 'straw', 'ber' and 'ry', for spelling.

Dictation

1. raw
2. claw
3. thaw
4. yawn
5. shawl
6. straw

1. I have drawn a picture.
2. The cows lay down on some straw.
3. Would you like some prawns?

Spelling List 36

1. zip
2. men
3. po**nd**
4. saw
5. claw
6. dawn
7. prawn
8. **mother**
9. **father**
10. strawberry

Write an ‹**aw**› word and draw a picture in each saw.

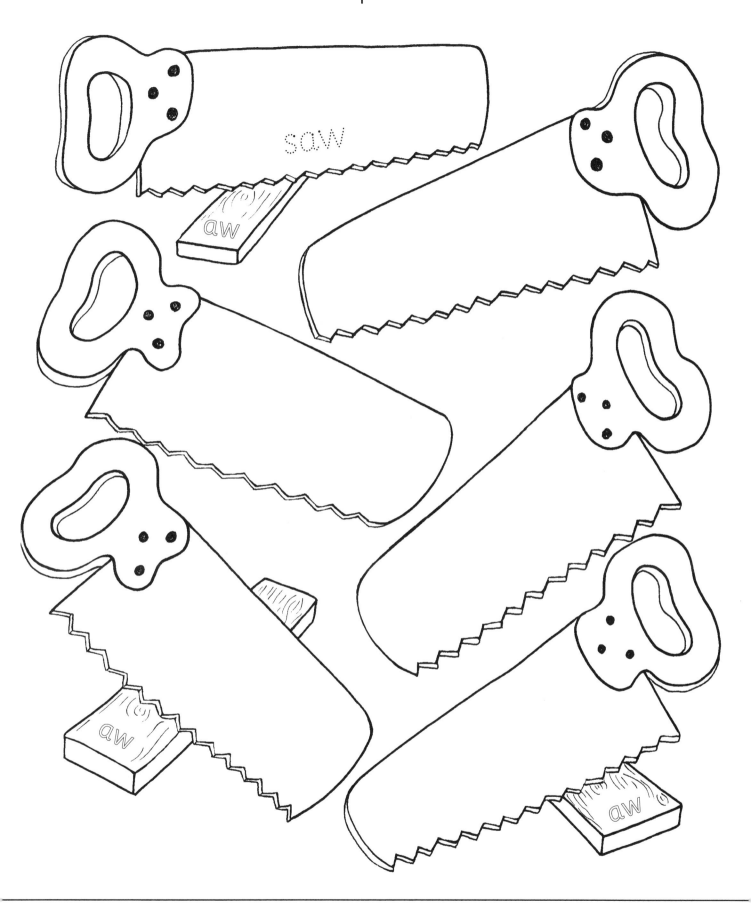

Action: Put hands on head as if donkey's ears pointing down, and say *or*. (This comes from the *ee or* action.)

Grammar 36 – Revision

Prepare...
Big book
(Acetate and pens)
Grammar sheet 36
(Jolly Grammar Big
Book 1)

Aim: Revise the parts of speech learnt so far.

Introduction: Revise proper nouns, common nouns and pronouns. Revise adjectives. Call out some nouns and ask the children to think of adjectives to describe them. Revise verbs. Conjugate a verb. Call out some verbs and ask the children to think of adverbs to describe them.

Main Point: This is a revision session, allowing the children to apply some of what have learnt to a piece of writing. Look at the last page in the *Jolly Grammar Big Book 1*. Alternatively you could choose a page from a big book you have. Read it with the children, identifying the parts of speech they have learnt. A large sheet of acetate could be placed over the page and used to underline the words in the appropriate colours.

Grammar sheet 36: With the children, read the story on the sheet. First the children write inside the word nouns in black, and underline all the nouns they can find. They then repeat for the verbs, underlining in red. It does not matter if the children do not find all the nouns and verbs, so long as they see some of them and show that they are beginning to understand how words work in sentences.

Extension activity: The children repeat the exercise, looking for the pronouns, adjectives and adverbs.

Rounding off: Go over the sheet with the children. (See answers below.)

Key: Noun^N Verb^V Pronoun^P Adjective^{Aj} Adverb^{Av}

'Inky^N works^V hard^{Av} in the garden^N. She^P digs^V the brown^{Aj} earth^N. The birds^N watch^V her interestedly^{Av}. They^P wait^V impatiently^{Av} for the worms^N.

In the Spring^N she^P plants^V the seeds^N in the ground^N. She^P grows^V orange^{Aj} carrots^N, crispy^{Aj} lettuces^N and tall^{Aj}, green^{Aj} beans^N. In Summer^N, she^P carefully^{Av} harvests^V the delicious^{Aj} vegetables^N and eats^V them.

She^P also grows^V tall^{Aj}, yellow^{Aj} sunflowers^N. She^P likes^V the beautiful^{Aj} sunflowers^N. The birds^N also^{Av} like^V the sunflowers^N. They^P hungrily^{Av} eat^V the striped^{Aj} black^{Aj} and white^{Aj} seeds^N.'

Underline the nouns in black and the verbs in red.

Inky works hard in the garden. She digs the brown earth. The birds watch her interestedly. They wait impatiently for the worms.

In the Spring she plants the seeds in the ground. She grows orange carrots, crispy lettuces and tall, green beans. In Summer, she carefully harvests the delicious vegetables and eats them.

She also grows tall, yellow sunflowers. She likes the beautiful sunflowers. The birds also like the sunflowers. They hungrily eat the striped black and white seeds.

 Pink    Blue    Orange

Pronouns   Adjectives   Adverbs

Now see if you can underline the pronouns in pink, the adjectives in blue and the adverbs in orange.

Photocopy Section 2

Master Sheets

Dictation Master (page 171)

This master may be photocopied onto the backs of the Spelling Sheets. It provides lines, for the children to write the dictation words and sentences.

Writing Master (page 172)

This master may be photocopied on to the backs of the Grammar Sheets when required. It provides extra lines, which the children may need for their writing.

Parts of Speech Master (page 173)

This master may be photocopied and enlarged to make a poster for display in the classroom. The names of the parts of speech are provided in outline, to be filled in with the appropriate colours.

Name: _____

Dictation

1. _____   2. _____

3. _____   4. _____

5. _____   6. _____

Sentences

1. _____

_____

2. _____

_____

3. _____

_____

Name: _____

Parts of Speech

Nouns ✏ Black

Pronouns ✏ Pink

Verbs ✏ Red

Adjectives ✏ Blue

Adverbs ✏ Orange

Photocopy Section 3

Flash Card Sheets

There are two sets of sheets which may be photocopied, cut up and stuck onto card to make flash cards.

Digraphs and Alternative Vowel Spellings (pages 175-80)

At this stage the children should already know the sounds made by the single alphabet letters. They will, however, take longer to master the digraphs (two letters which make a single sound), and will need to learn the alternative ways of spelling vowel sounds. Go through the flash cards as often as possible.

Consonant Blends (pages 181-85)

It is difficult for the children to hear the individual sounds in consonant blends (clusters of two or more consonants). It is useful for the children to know these blends well.

The children read unfamiliar words with greater ease once they can blend consonants together fluently, instead of sounding out each one on its own, e.g. '**fl**-a-g', not 'f-l-a-g'. Hold up the flash card for the children to say the blend.

For writing, the children need to be aware of the individual sounds in a blend. They often write a word such as 'flag' as 'fag' because they do not hear the second sound in the blend. This problem can be overcome with regular practice. Call out blends, for the children to say the individual sounds, holding up a finger for each one as they say it, e.g. for 'fl' they say '/f/, /l/' showing two fingers, and for 'scr' they say '/s/,/c/,/r/,' showing three fingers.

It is helpful for the children to think of examples of words with the blends in too.

sh

ch

th

ng

qu

ar

ff

ll

ss

zz

ck

wh

a_e   i_e

o_e   u_e

ay   ea

igh

y

ow

ew

ou

oi

oy

or

al

er

ir

ur

nk

au

aw

cl

bl

fl

gl

pl

sl

br

cr

dr	fr
gr	pr
tr	sc
sm	sn

sw	tw
sk	sp
nt	st
lb	ld

lf

lk

lm

lp

lt

ct

ft

pt

xt	mp
nd	spl
spr	str
scr	squ

Photocopy Section 4

Spelling and Tricky Word Sheets

Spelling List Sheets (pages 187-93)

Each week the children have a list of ten spelling words to take home and learn. The six Spelling List Sheets (pages 188-193) provide all the spelling lists ready to be photocopied, cut up and stuck into the children's spelling homework books. To encourage parents to help their child, a parents' advice sheet (page 187) has been provided. This can be copied, cut and stuck at the front of the spelling homework books. When the spelling tests have been marked, the results can be written into each book, to indicate to the parents how well their child has done.

Two tricky words are included in the weekly spelling list. However, it is useful to go over the tricky words separately as well. Two types of sheet are provided for extra practice.

Tricky Words Spelling List Sheet (page 194)

The Tricky Word Spelling Lists group together the twelve tricky words from each six weeks. They may be photocopied, cut up and given out, as an extra spelling homework, either in the holidays, or if there are any weeks to spare.

'Look, Copy, Cover, Write and Check' (pages 195-200)

The 'Look, Copy, Cover, Write, Check' method is an effective way for the children to learn to spell tricky words. There is one sheet for each set of twelve tricky words. These can either be used in school, or given to the children to take home.

Parents' Advice Sheet

Dear Parent or Guardian,

Each week your child will be given ten spellings. Please help him/her to learn them.

Most of the spelling words are regular. These can be spelt by listening for the sounds and writing the letter(s) for them.

The eighth and ninth words are irregular or tricky, and have to be learnt by heart. Once your child knows the names for all the letters in the alphabet, he/she can learn these harder words by saying the names of the letters in them, e.g. for the word 'the', your child should say 'tee aitch ee' several times each day until the word is known.

Dear Parent or Guardian,

Each week your child will be given ten spellings. Please help him/her to learn them.

Most of the spelling words are regular. These can be spelt by listening for the sounds and writing the letter(s) for them.

The eighth and ninth words are irregular or tricky, and have to be learnt by heart. Once your child knows the names for all the letters in the alphabet, he/she can learn these harder words by saying the names of the letters in them, e.g. for the word 'the', your child should say 'tee aitch ee' several times each day until the word is known.

Dear Parent or Guardian,

Each week your child will be given ten spellings. Please help him/her to learn them.

Most of the spelling words are regular. These can be spelt by listening for the sounds and writing the letter(s) for them.

The eighth and ninth words are irregular or tricky, and have to be learnt by heart. Once your child knows the names for all the letters in the alphabet, he/she can learn these harder words by saying the names of the letters in them, e.g. for the word 'the', your child should say 'tee aitch ee' several times each day until the word is known.

Dear Parent or Guardian,

Each week your child will be given ten spellings. Please help him/her to learn them.

Most of the spelling words are regular. These can be spelt by listening for the sounds and writing the letter(s) for them.

The eighth and ninth words are irregular or tricky, and have to be learnt by heart. Once your child knows the names for all the letters in the alphabet, he/she can learn these harder words by saying the names of the letters in them, e.g. for the word 'the', your child should say 'tee aitch ee' several times each day until the word is known.

Dear Parent or Guardian,

Each week your child will be given ten spellings. Please help him/her to learn them.

Most of the spelling words are regular. These can be spelt by listening for the sounds and writing the letter(s) for them.

The eighth and ninth words are irregular or tricky, and have to be learnt by heart. Once your child knows the names for all the letters in the alphabet, he/she can learn these harder words by saying the names of the letters in them, e.g. for the word 'the', your child should say 'tee aitch ee' several times each day until the word is known.

Dear Parent or Guardian,

Each week your child will be given ten spellings. Please help him/her to learn them.

Most of the spelling words are regular. These can be spelt by listening for the sounds and writing the letter(s) for them.

The eighth and ninth words are irregular or tricky, and have to be learnt by heart. Once your child knows the names for all the letters in the alphabet, he/she can learn these harder words by saying the names of the letters in them, e.g. for the word 'the', your child should say 'tee aitch ee' several times each day until the word is known.

Spelling Lists 1-6

1.

sh

1. am
2. get
3. clap
4. shop
5. fish
6. shut
7. wish
8. I
9. the
10. shampoo

2.

ch

1. if
2. hot
3. blot
4. chips
5. lunch
6. chest
7. much
8. he
9. she
10. chicken

3.

th

1. us
2. sad
3. flag
4. this
5. with
6. that
7. thank
8. me
9. we
10. thinking

4.

ng

1. in
2. leg
3. glad
4. ring
5. sang
6. strong
7. lung
8. be
9. was
10. length

5.

qu

1. on
2. but
3. plum
4. quick
5. quiz
6. queen
7. squid
8. to
9. do
10. squirrel

6.

ar

1. at
2. yes
3. slug
4. arm
5. hard
6. scarf
7. card
8. are
9. all
10. farmyard

Spelling Lists 7-12

7. Days
1. dog
2. bran
3. Monday
4. Tuesday
5. Wednesday
6. Thursday
7. Friday
8. you
9. your
10. Saturday

8. ff
1. up
2. man
3. crab
4. off
5. cliff
6. stiff
7. cuff
8. come
9. some
10. stuffing

9. ll
1. red
2. win
3. drum
4. will
5. bell
6. doll
7. skull
8. said
9. here
10. windmill

10. ss / zz
1. ox
2. run
3. from
4. buzz
5. cross
6. less
7. miss
8. there
9. they
10. crossroad

11. ck
1. hop
2. fit
3. grin
4. duck
5. neck
6. clock
7. lick
8. go
9. no
10. broomstick

12. y at end
1. bed
2. wet
3. prod
4. holly
5. party
6. story
7. happy
8. so
9. my
10. family

Spelling Lists 13-18

13. Colours

1. sad
2. let
3. trip
4. blue
5. orange
6. grey
7. black
8. one
9. by
10. colour

14. a_e

1. ran
2. hat
3. scarf
4. came
5. grape
6. name
7. cake
8. only
9. old
10. pavement

15. i_e

1. six
2. hat
3. smell
4. bike
5. time
6. smile
7. prize
8. like
9. have
10. bridesmaid

16. o_e

1. cod
2. lot
3. snap
4. bone
5. nose
6. home
7. globe
8. live
9. give
10. tadpole

17. u_e

1. bus
2. pot
3. swim
4. cube
5. tune
6. used
7. excuse
8. little
9. down
10. useless

18. wh

1. did
2. cut
3. twin
4. whale
5. wheel
6. white
7. whisper
8. what
9. when
10. whenever

Spelling Lists 19-24

19.

ay

1. an
2. cat
3. skin
4. say
5. away
6. play
7. today
8. why
9. where
10. playground

20.

ea

1. met
2. web
3. spin
4. tea
5. heat
6. leaf
7. each
8. who
9. which
10. seaside

21.

igh

1. lip
2. his
3. went
4. night
5. high
6. might
7. light
8. any
9. many
10. frightening

22.

y

1. win
2. sit
3. stop
4. fry
5. dry
6. crying
7. sky
8. more
9. before
10. myself

23.

ow

1. box
2. job
3. bulb
4. own
5. grow
6. elbow
7. yellow
8. other
9. were
10. snowman

24.

ew

1. bud
2. sun
3. held
4. few
5. flew
6. grew
7. chew
8. because
9. want
10. newspaper

Spelling Lists 25-30

25. ou

1. bat
2. pet
3. self
4. out
5. our
6. round
7. mouth
8. saw
9. put
10. outside

26. ow

1. big
2. fox
3. milk
4. how
5. owl
6. brown
7. town
8. could
9. should
10. flowerpot

27. oi

1. bug
2. had
3. film
4. oil
5. coin
6. noisy
7. toilet
8. would
9. right
10. boiling

28. oy

1. jet
2. dig
3. help
4. boy
5. toy
6. enjoy
7. annoy
8. two
9. four
10. destroy

29. or

1. got
2. bun
3. belt
4. fork
5. storm
6. horse
7. forty
8. goes
9. does
10. morning

30. al

1. bad
2. vet
3. fact
4. all
5. talk
6. walk
7. small
8. made
9. their
10. beanstalk

Spelling Lists 31-36

31.

nk

1. fin
2. sob
3. left
4. sink
5. pink
6. drink
7. think
8. once
9. upon
10. thinking

32.

er

1. mud
2. jam
3. sent
4. term
5. summer
6. river
7. number
8. always
9. also
10. woodpecker

33.

ir

1. yet
2. hid
3. wept
4. skirt
5. girl
6. shirt
7. first
8. of
9. eight
10. birthday

34.

ur

1. not
2. sum
3. next
4. turn
5. nurse
6. turkey
7. purple
8. love
9. cover
10. hamburger

35.

au

1. map
2. fix
3. jump
4. fault
5. autumn
6. haunt
7. August
8. after
9. every
10. astronaut

36.

aw

1. zip
2. men
3. pond
4. saw
5. claw
6. dawn
7. prawn
8. mother
9. father
10. strawberry

Tricky Word Spelling Lists

1. I	13. you	25. one
2. the	14. your	26. by
3. he	15. come	27. only
4. she	16. some	28. old
5. me	17. said	29. like
6. we	18. here	30. have
7. be	19. there	31. live
8. was	20. they	32. give
9. to	21. go	33. little
10. do	22. no	34. down
11. are	23. so	35. what
12. all	24. my	36. when
37. why	49. saw	61. once
38. where	50. put	62. upon
39. who	51. could	63. always
40. which	52. should	64. also
41. any	53. would	65. of
42. many	54. right	66. eight
43. more	55. two	67. love
44. before	56. four	68. cover
45. other	57. goes	69. after
46. were	58. does	70. every
47. because	59. made	71. mother
48. want	60. their	72. father

Look Say the letter names.	**Copy** Try writing the word. **Cover**	**Write** **Check** Is it right?	Have another go!
I	_____	_____	_____
the	_____	_____	_____
he	_____	_____	_____
she	_____	_____	_____
me	_____	_____	_____
we	_____	_____	_____
be	_____	_____	_____
was	_____	_____	_____
to	_____	_____	_____
do	_____	_____	_____
are	_____	_____	_____
all	_____	_____	_____

Look	Copy	Write	Have another go!
Say the letter names.	Try writing the word. **Cover**	**Check** Is it right? 	

you

your

come

some

said

here

there

they

go

no

so

my

Look Say the letter names.	**Copy** Try writing the word. **Cover**	**Write** **Check** Is it right?	Have another go!
one	_____	_____	_____
by	_____	_____	_____
only	_____	_____	_____
old	_____	_____	_____
like	_____	_____	_____
have	_____	_____	_____
live	_____	_____	_____
give	_____	_____	_____
little	_____	_____	_____
down	_____	_____	_____
what	_____	_____	_____
when	_____	_____	_____

Look Say the letter names.	**Copy** Try writing the word. **Cover**	**Write** **Check** Is it right?	Have another go!
why	_____	_____	_____
where	_____	_____	_____
who	_____	_____	_____
which	_____	_____	_____
any	_____	_____	_____
many	_____	_____	_____
more	_____	_____	_____
before	_____	_____	_____
other	_____	_____	_____
were	_____	_____	_____
because	_____	_____	_____
want	_____	_____	_____

Look Say the letter names.	Copy Try writing the word. **Cover**	Write **Check** Is it right?	Have another go!
saw	_____	_____	_____
put	_____	_____	_____
could	_____	_____	_____
should	_____	_____	_____
would	_____	_____	_____
right	_____	_____	_____
two	_____	_____	_____
four	_____	_____	_____
goes	_____	_____	_____
does	_____	_____	_____
made	_____	_____	_____
their	_____	_____	_____

Look Say the letter names.	Copy Try writing the word. **Cover**	Write **Check** Is it right?	Have another go!
once	_____	_____	_____
upon	_____	_____	_____
always	_____	_____	_____
also	_____	_____	_____
of	_____	_____	_____
eight	_____	_____	_____
love	_____	_____	_____
cover	_____	_____	_____
after	_____	_____	_____
every	_____	_____	_____
mother	_____	_____	_____
father	_____	_____	_____

Photocopy Section 5

Alphabet Sheets

The children need to become thoroughly familiar with the order of the alphabet, as so many reference materials are organised in alphabetical order. There are two types of sheet provided for extra practice.

Alphabet Letter Sets (pages 202-3)

These sheets may be photocopied and cut up to make sets of capital and lower-case alphabet letters. The sets can be used in a number of ways:

a. Give each child a letter, asking them to say its name and/or sound.

b. Give a child a complete set of capital or lower-case letters to arrange in alphabetical order (see Grammar 1, pages 28-9, and Grammar 4, pages 40-41).

c. Give a child a complete set of capital or lower-case letters to arrange into the four dictionary groups (see Grammar 7, pages 52-3 and the *Jolly Dictionary)*. These are the groups into which the letters would fall if a dictionary was divided into four approximately-equal parts:

   1. Aa Bb Cc Dd Ee (‹E› falls a quarter of the way through)
   2. Ff Gg Hh Ii Jj Kk Ll Mm (‹M› falls halfway through)
   3. Nn Oo Pp Qq Rr Ss (‹S› is three quarters of the way through)
   4. Tt Uu Vv Ww Xx Yy Zz.

d. Sit the children in a circle and give each of them a letter. Call out a regular word. Those children, whose letters are in the word, use them to spell the word in the middle of the circle. This is also a good way of practising the tricky words.

Alphabet Writing Card (page 204)

This sheet may be photocopied, stuck onto card and laminated. A piece of tracing paper may be clipped to the card, for a child to practise writing out the alphabet (See Grammar 4, pages 40-41).

Alphabet Letter Set – Lower-case

a	b	c	d
e	f	g	h
i	j	k	l
m	n	o	p
q	r	s	t
u	v	w	x
y	z		

Alphabet Letter Set – Capitals

A	B	C	D
E	F	G	H
I	J	K	L
M	N	O	P
Q	R	S	T
U	V	W	X
Y	Z		

Aa Bb Cc Dd Ee Ff

Gg Hh Ii Jj Kk Ll

Mm Nn Oo Pp Qq

Rr Ss Tt Uu Vv

Ww Xx Yy Zz

'Sentence Sticking' Sheets

The 'Sentence Sticking' Sheets can be used with Grammar sheet 2 (page 33), so that the children do not all have the same sentence to unscramble. Alternatively the sheets can be used as an extension activity. Each pair of sentence sticking exercises is harder than the one before.

The

are

hopping.

rabbits

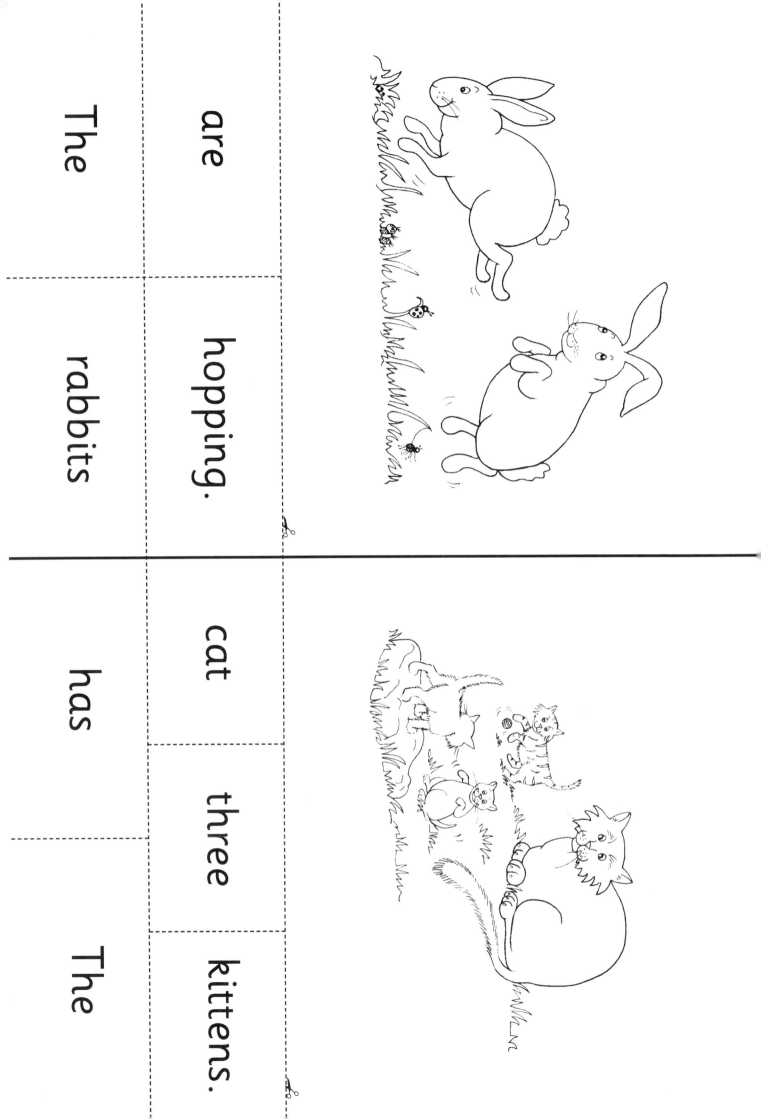

cat

has

three

The

kittens.

nest.	run
The	to
chicks	the
very	red
dirty.	is
tractor	The

swings	slide	
There	in	
the	and	park.
	are	a

she	buzzed	from
the	collected	flowers.
	as	pollen
	The	Bee

Photocopy Section 7

'Pull-Out Plurals' Sheet

This sheet can be used as a fun extension activity. The children choose a noun and draw a picture for it in the top frame. Then they draw two or more pictures of the same thing in the second frame. They cut out both pieces, cut the slits as indicated, and fit the two pieces together. They have to cut very carefully to make 'pull-out plural' work. This exercise offers the children a multisensory way to understand the concept of plurals (see Grammar 9, pages 60-61).

Pull-Out Plurals

Draw something in the top frame.
Draw more than one of the same thing in the lower frame.
Cut out the 2 pieces. Cut the slits in the rectangle.
Put in your pull-out plural.

Singular

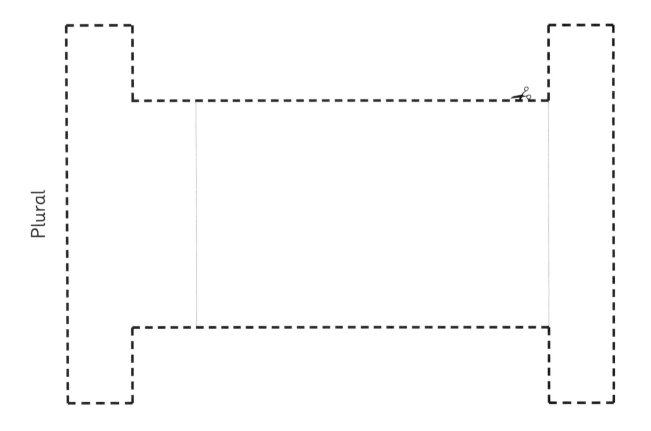

Plural

'Verb Bees' Sheet

The children can use this big bee shape to make their own 'busy verb bees'.

The outlined bee shape may be photocopied, or used to make a card template. The children each choose a verb, and then add wings, legs, etc. to show their bee performing it. They can look at the bees on Grammar sheet 14 (page 81), and the bees on the Verbs page in the *Jolly Grammar Big Book 1,* for ideas. The big bees can then be used to make a verb display.

Photocopy Section 9

'Adjective Snake' Sheets

The outlined snake sections may be photocopied for the children to make 'adjective snakes,' either in groups or individually. Any number of middle (body) sections can be used between the snake's head and tail.

The children colour each body section of the snake in a different way, and write or stick on an adjective (e.g. 'red', 'sad', 'scaly', 'spotty') to describe it. (See the snakes on Grammar sheet 21, page 109, and the Adjectives page in the *Jolly Grammar Big Book 1*, for ideas.) The sections may be stuck together to make an 'adjective snake' for display.

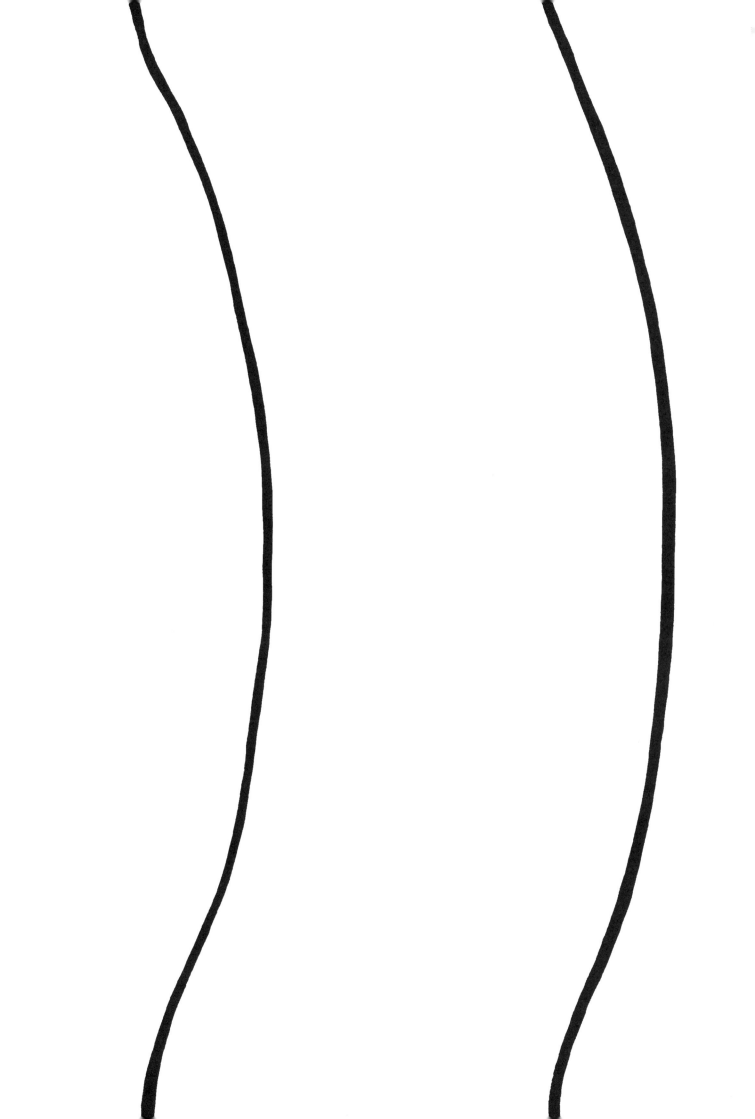

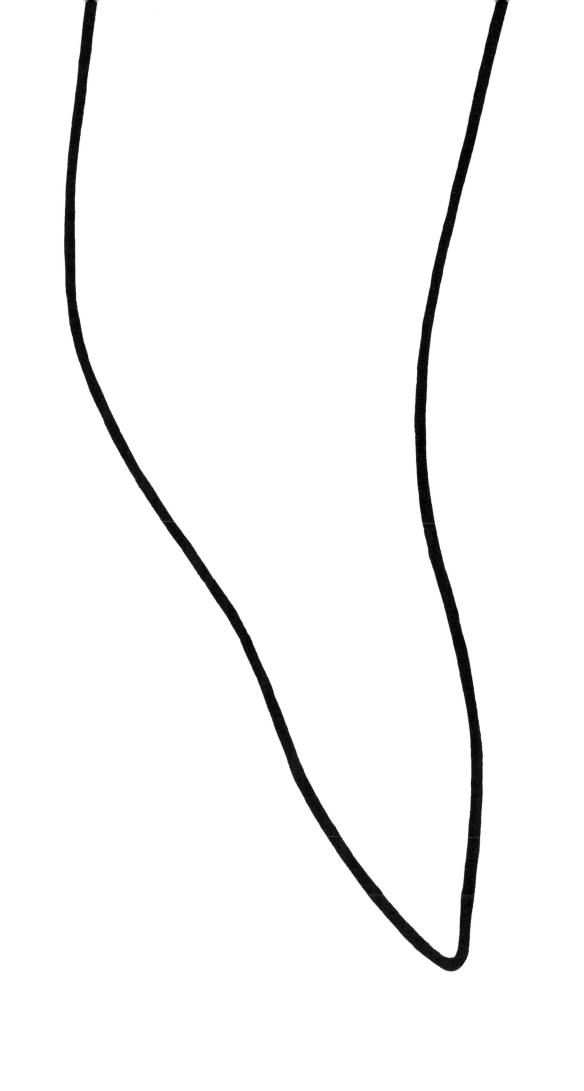

'Compound Birds' Sheet

The 'compound birds' sheet may be photocopied and cut up to make sets of compound word puzzles. Use the photocopier to enlarge them if preferred. Then write the the first part of a compound word on the head, and the second part on the tail, of each bird. (See Grammar sheet 24 on page 121, and the Compound Words page of the *Jolly Grammar Big Book 1*, for ideas.) Muddle up the pieces and see if the children can match the birds with their tails, by reading the words.

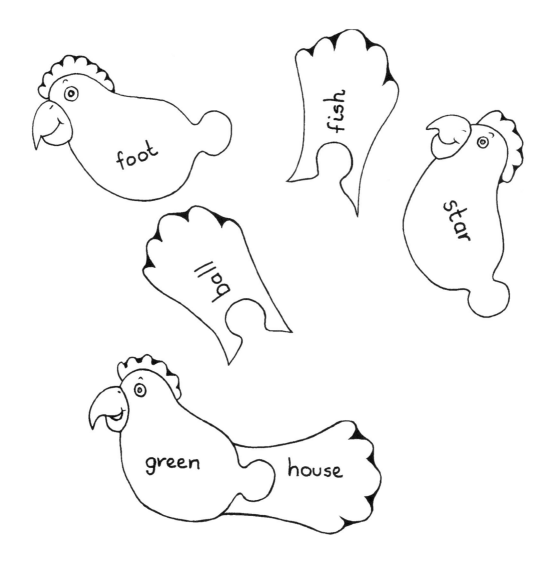

Compound Birds

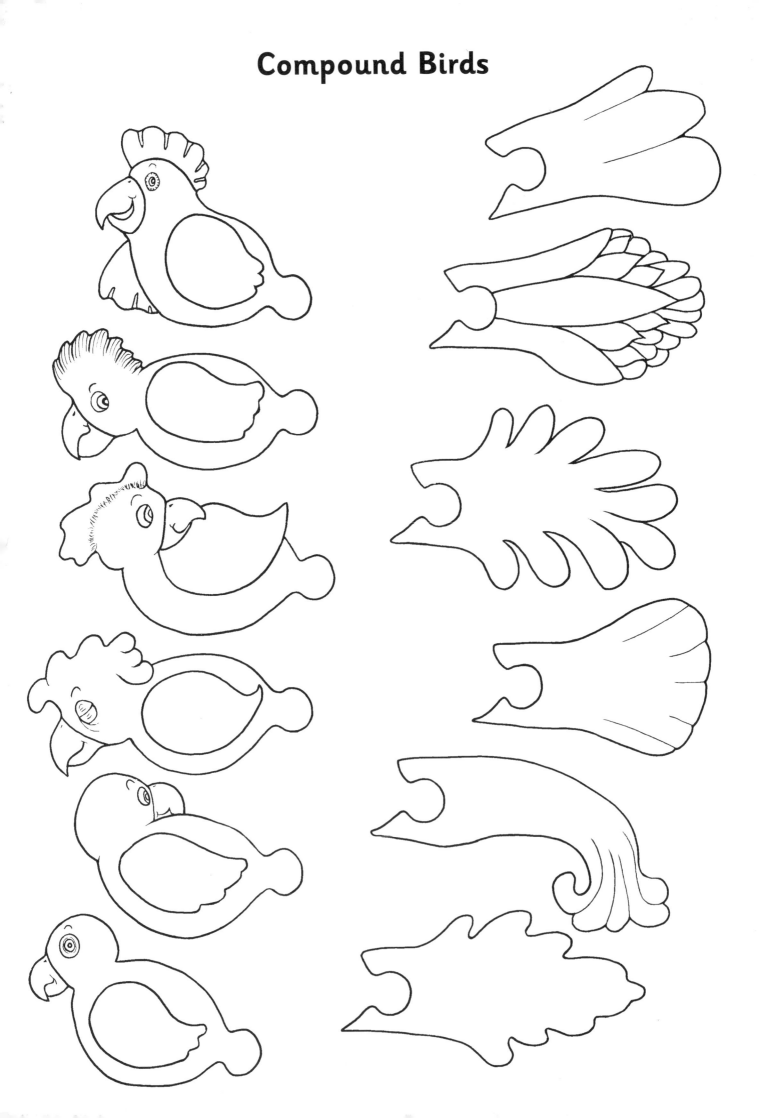